SISTER MAY.

A Novel.

BY THE
AUTHOR OF "MARGARET'S ENGAGEMENT," "MY
INSECT QUEEN," &c.

"The high that proved too high, the heroic for earth too hard,
  The passion that left the ground to lose itself in the sky;
Are music sent up to GOD by the lover and the bard;
  Enough that He heard it once; we shall hear it by-and-by."
ABT VOGLER.

IN THREE VOLUMES.
VOL. I.

LONDON:
RICHARD BENTLEY AND SON,
NEW BURLINGTON STREET.
1871.

CONTENTS OF VOL. I.

I.—SYBIL'S PORTION.

CONTENTS.

SISTER MAY.

I.—SYBIL'S PORTION.

CHAPTER I.

GOOD-BYE TO THE SCHOOLROOM.

"MAY!—sweet sister May!—have you forgotten what day it is?"

When Sybil asked me this question, I was busily employed in arranging on a book-shelf certain volumes, chiefly useful for the instruction of youth—books which had been presented to me, ten years ago, by thoughtful friends, when, little more than a girl myself, I had assumed the

duties of preceptress of the young ladies'
seminary in quiet, dull, old-fashioned Bedford Square.

These volumes, with divers other odds
and ends likely to prove useful to her, I
destined for a parting gift to my dear Miss
Colvin, my quondam governess—later, my
coadjutrix—and now, my successor in the
establishment which, on the morrow, I
should quit for ever. Certainly I was not
sorry to leave Bedford Square, and never
since I went there had the dim future
smiled so brightly on me as now ; and yet
I lingered with something of a tender
regret over each book as I ranged it on the
shelf—the half-regret we feel in looking
back on the past, when the quiet seems
rest, which we called gloom while we dwelt
in it.

Thus dreaming, I did not answer my

little sister's question, and she repeated it, with a playful imperiousness that, at any other time, would have incurred a reproof from Miss Colvin, who was seated at a desk making an inventory of Laura Tresham's belongings—Laura, the last lingering swallow of our brood, who was to take wing for her distant home in Cornwall to-morrow.

"May—May!" repeated Sybil, "have you forgotten what day it is?"

Thus urged, I looked round, with a volume of Gibbon in my hand.

"No, dear, of course not—it is the 7th of April, 18——"

"We know that; but it is a memory, not a date, that I am asking of you."

"A memory, Sybil?—and belonging to this day? Well, yes, to be sure—it is your birthday. I did remember it this morning, and I gave you——"

"Oh! you mean thing!—as if my birthday was only to be remembered by a gift!"

And Sybil flung a little paper pellet at me—a breach of decorum which was too much for Miss Colvin's forbearance.

"Miss Wharnecliffe!—Sybil! You are getting quite a romp! She is over-excited by the joy of leaving us all!" and there was a tone of pathetic reproach in my old friend's voice, though she smiled, too, at the consciousness of being at that moment the sole representative of "us all"—for Laura also was leaving school "for good."

Sybil laughed, and gave her a loving little pat on the head—a greater freedom, I am sure, than throwing a paper pellet at me; but Miss Colvin did not seem disposed to resent it.

"Now, I won't be scolded, though you

are Lady Preceptress, and Commander—
(do you say Commander, or Commandress ?)
—in-Chief ! I am leaving school, and I
may say what I like ; and May is my sister
only, henceforth, and not Lady Preceptress
any longer ; and I choose to remind her of
a promise she once made me for to-day—
which she chooses to pretend to have forgotten."

" Indeed, I remember no promise, my
love."

" There, Laura ! Did I not tell you she
would say she had forgotten it ?"

" But I really have, dear. I will fulfil
it, if you will only tell me what it was."

" You promised me—not once, but many
times—that when I should be a woman,
and leaving school for good, you would tell
me all the story of your life—before I was
born, and before we came to live here. It

should be on a fête day, you said, and I should bring with me, to listen to it, my dearest, most trusted friend. Now I claim your promised story! I leave school to-morrow, for good. Here" (pointing to Miss Tresham) "is my dearest friend, and I am a woman, certainly, for I am sixteen to-day."

Yes, I had made that promise, it is true, but the conditions implied were scarcely yet fulfilled. I had dreamt of a "leaving school for good," very different from this. I could not then know that a distant and unseen relative would one day die and leave me independent, and the "trusted friend" I pictured as bearing my young sister away from school, was very unlike the object of her girlish devotion as yet. Little gipsy! I believe she knew this as well as I did, for there was a sly twinkle in her bright eyes as she turned from Laura to me, and a mischievous archness in the dimples round her mouth, that belied her affected demureness, though it quite " took in " poor Miss Colvin. However, of course I did not betray any suspicion, and answered, quite innocently—

" Well, child, I will tell you the story if you wish it ; it is not much to tell, but it is an odd time to choose, when we have been so busy all the day. Laura looks tired, and Miss Colvin and I have ever so many things to do yet."

" That is just what it is !" rejoined my persecutor gaily, "you have been a great deal too busy, considering that it is my birthday, which only comes once a year, and which you should have devoted to me, as you always have done until to-day. We are all tired, of course, and we want to be amused ; there is nothing more to be done, or if there is, there will be time enough to-morrow. Our

train does not start till eleven. So now
leave off all this rummaging, and come out
of this empty, echoing schoolroom into the
parlour, and order tea, and sit over the fire ;
and you shall begin at the beginning and
tell us all your story. Oh, Laura! she can
tell a story so prettily ; she used to tell me
lovely stories when we were too poor to
afford a sea-side trip in the holidays, and she
wanted to amuse me when we were left alone
together, and this story will be the best of
all, because it will be true."

Sybil's request was eagerly seconded by
Laura Tresham, and even Miss Colvin declared that she thought it would be a fitting
termination to this, the last day of our
school life. So we adjourned to the parlour,
I pausing, as we went, to cast one lingering
look of adieu, round the empty " class-room "
littered all over with the rubbish of packing—

loose straws, and torn paper and little heaps
of cast-away scraps, looking so untidy and
desolate, with its carpetless floor and com-
fortless desks, and long rows of vacant
benches, where, but a few days since, it was
all alive with the restless movement of lithe
girlish figures, and musical with the murmur of sweet girlish voices, like the hum of
honey bees, in "academic groves." Only
our groves were so leafless!

Poor old school-room! some of us have
been very happy in you, yet, ungrateful that
we are, we are very glad to leave you for
ever. Even I, the mistress and queen of
this little kingdom, can abdicate my rule
without a sigh! Good bye, dingy old school-
room!

The parlour is better, that is to say, it is
finer. Quite elegantly furnished, and deco-
rated with beautiful drawings, done by my

various pupils at different times. Beautiful
drawings—at least, they have beautiful
frames—and really at a distance looked
almost as well as if they had been done by
the first masters. Though, of course, it
depended upon the distance from which they
were contemplated. But they looked very
nice, if you were not too critical as to trifling
points, such as an occasional fault in perspec-
tive, or a little too bright a blue in the water,
or yellow in the sky. Then there were couches
and easy chairs, richly embroidered in silk
and velvet, with cushions all glittering with
bead-work, that was charming to look at;
but the beads were hard to lean against, and
rubbed off on the back of your dress—and
there were vases of wax-flowers, just like
real ones, only they had no wavering motion
and no fragrant breath, and grew monotonous in a few days, because they wouldn't

fade ! Sometimes when they were on the mantle-piece, and the room was very hot, I have known one or two to collapse suddenly —a poppy did once—all its petals fell off, and there was a hideous bit of scarlet wire, sticking up in the midst of the bouquet ever after, like a blood-stained thorn.

Then there were books, splendidly bound in crimson and gold, and "illuminated titles," which were so undecipherable, that they were anything but illuminations of the subject. But the books were chiefly such as everyone knows by heart, and I, for one, infinitely preferred my little old worn edition of " The Christian Year " or "In Memoriam," where I could almost lay my finger in the dark on any favourite passage,—to the gaudy, bedizened editions, that lay on the table, well nigh too splendid to touch ! Beautiful books, like beautiful faces, may attract

strangers by costly adornments, but are fairest
to those who love them, in their homeliest,
most familiar dress.

And all these treasures had been presented
to me by my pupils or their parents, in token
of esteem and affection for my proper person;
but I looked on them, in fact, as honorary
prizes—testimonials to the efficiency of my
school.   They were the regalia of my throne
—the heirlooms of my estate, and as such,
I bequeathed them all to my successor in
office, Jane Colvin, to whom indeed, quite
as much as to me, belonged the merit of such
prosperity as we had achieved.   So I left
her all, except a few "unconsidered trifles"
that had been given me at parting, by some
of my pupil teachers, who were too poor to
afford costlier remembrances, when they
left me for better situations.   I retained,
besides, a little Church Service, bound in

velvet, and clasped with silver, on the fly-
leaf of which was written, in a childish hand,
" *Fanny Brereton, from her darling Papa.*"

And under this was inscribed in a man's
writing—

" *To May Wharnecliffe, in memory of
little Fanny, from a grateful father.*"

Poor little Fanny, she was one of the first
pupils I ever had, and the youngest. She
was only eight when she died. Captain
Brereton had given me too a little gold locket,
with a curl of soft hair in it. These I kept ;
all the rest I gave to Jane Colvin, and they
formed, as they had always done, the deco-
rations of our state parlour, when we assembled for the last time to tea.

Stay—I have described the room—let me
now describe its inmates.

First, Miss Colvin, a quiet, decorous little
maiden lady, about fifty years old. Not un-

comely was Jane Colvin, with her quaint,
stiff little figure, always plainly attired, but
with scrupulous neatness and propriety ; her
gray hair smoothed under a lace cap, always
trimmed with white ribbons, her Quaker gray
silk dress and black mittens on her hands,
which were invariably very blue in winter,
and very red in summer, and a pervading
tint of grayness all over her prim, diminu·
tive person, like—-what shall I say ? like one
of those silvery plants which are so fashionable for the edging of gay flower-beds—No,
I think she was more like one of those "ever-
lasting" flowers, which look wonderfully well
preserved and crisp, but which never could
have boasted any real bloom or freshness
—else why should Jenny Colvin not look
young still, instead of merely not looking
old ? Her features were regular, her complexion smooth and clear. Her eyes, of a

cold gray, could never have faded to that
tint from blue. There were no lines or
wrinkles in her face. Time seldom draws
many when he has not used the " iron nail "
of thought or passion, and unless perhaps
for her hair, I do not know how Jane could
have looked very different at eighteen from
what she looked at fifty. At least, she never
looked different to me when she came to be
my governess, when I was quite a little girl,
and she must have been almost young then.

But, if " a thing of beauty is a joy for
ever," it must be a joy for ever to remember
Sybil at sixteen, for I am sure that nothing
more exquisitely lovely ever breathed in
female form. She is but middle height,
though taller than Miss Colvin, and very
tall compared to me. But then I am such
a crumb. " Mayette," my mother used to
call me; " Miette," and " Mite," are my play-

ful pseudonyms now. But it is only as measured by me, that Sybil can be considered tall, and her figure shows by its full and rounded contour that she has attained her utmost height. Her low white forehead, her straight nose with its delicate nostril, and the curve of the short upper lip, are so purely Greek and statuesque, that one wonders to see them in the face of an English girl. But the dark chesnut brown hair is quite English; and so is the healthy bloom of the complexion—too fair for a brunette, too ripely coloured for a blonde. Then, the deep blue eyes, with their pencilled brows, and long lashes, and their sidelong, upward glance, half playful, half shy, but with the innocent candour of a child's. And the arch dimples that wake in the sweet frank smile, or sleep in the rounded chin, and the little white teeth like pearls, just seen between the scarlet threads of the slightly parted lips. Surely this was a face of perfect loveliness? It expressed, perhaps, no great intellectual power, no great capacity for deep thought or feeling. But there was a loving sweetness in it, a feminine sensibility, and above all, a virgin freshness and purity that gave the exquisite features their crowning grace.

Laura Tresham, Sybil's great friend, was two years older, but had not yet outgrown her girlish angularities of form, and though there were latent possibilities of beauty in her face, they were as yet undeveloped, or obscured by a general condition of freckles and untidiness, and a languor, the result of delicacy of constitution.

We were a happy little party, that evening—the girls, rejoicing in their glad future of freedom and enjoyment—and I too, rejoicing in my emancipation from duties in which I had never taken much pleasure, and with a secret joy of which my companions knew nothing, making low music in my inmost soul. Miss Colvin too—demure as she looked—sorry as I am sure she was, to part with my sister and me, was by no means insensible to the glory and honour of being the real head of the now thriving seminary in Bedford Square, an honour which, with all accruing profits, I had gladly made over to her, for old love's sake, without charge or fee, and which she, with her limited views of life, bounded as a nun's by her convent walls, considered the proudest fortune that could have befallen her in her fondest dreams.

The tea things having been removed, the girls arranged a cosy seat for me on the sofa, well propped up with cushions, and with the best footstool under my feet. Miss

Colvin had never in her life unbent to such enervating luxuries. The utmost relaxation she ever permitted herself was a low sewing chair, with a high straight back, and a seat that for softness or elasticity, might have been stuffed with old horse shoes; and on this she seated herself opposite to me, with her little blue hands folded on her knee, her little foot beating a measured tattoo on the hearth-rug, and a chill smile in one corner of her mouth (she never used both sides of her mouth in smiling, perhaps that made it last longer). Laura Tresham stood behind her, leaning on the back of her chair, and Sybil took up her favourite position at my feet, her head on my knee, and one of my hands, which she had drawn round her neck, clasped in both of hers. " Now, May," said she.

CHAPTER II.

A MERE SKETCH.

"A M I to begin with my earliest memories, Sybil? they are not very
cheerful ones, but happily they are also very
dim.   My father, an army surgeon, died in
India, when I was a mere baby, and my
mother returned with me to England,
widowed, friendless, and poor, with no
resource but a slender pension, barely sufficient to support her in a quiet country village.   Your father (*our* father, Sybil) was
the curate of a neighbouring parish, and the
similarity of surname, not a common one,

either, brought him to seek my mother's acquaintance, in the expectation of finding in her a relative. It proved merely a coincidence, however; if there was any relationship at all, it was too distant to trace, so before long it was merged in the nearer tie of marriage, for my mother was young and fair, and though her second husband was many years older than herself, he was so good and kind, so generous to her, so tender to me, that she could not have failed to love him. I do not remember their marriage. I can just remember our removal to Elmsley Parsonage three years later, when my poor mother faded away and died."

I paused, and Sybil lifted her head, and gazed at me with a bewildered look. "But May," she said, "my mamma did not die so, why, I was not born then!"

"My darling, your parents were mine by

affection but not by blood. So precious is
the bond of kindred, that I have never yet
cared to tell you this. But there is no true
cause for concealing what one day or other
you must have known."

Sybil's clear eyes still dwelt wistfully on
mine, then she gave a little sigh, and laid
her head down on my lap again. I went
on.

" My real father had had few relations.
I had none on either side who cared to
enquire for me, but the desolation of such
an orphanage was more than compensated
to me, by the wealth of love that was
lavished on me by my step-father, and by
the sweet and gentle woman whom he married a few years after my mother's death.
You were an autumn blossom, lassie. I had
reached my sixteenth year, and they were
still childless, they looked on me as their

own daughter, and had announced me to the world as their destined heiress, for those were my days of prosperity, children."

"Ah," cried Laura, "then you were rich once! The girls always said you were rich and grand, living in good style, and never intended to be worried with a school; but some of them thought that could not be, because even Sybil never heard you speak of it."

Sybil lifted her head again, with a petulant movement. "May never spoke to me at all of her young days, Laura; you see she never told me the least thing about herself."

"My dears," interposed Miss Colvin, "I am sure that Miss Wharnecliffe's reserve was prompted only by the most thoughtful kindness to her sister; she feared, by dwelling on the more prosperous past, to discontent her with the more laborious future that lay before her.　Now that prosperous days have come back, Sybil——"

Sybil broke forth reproachfully, "Am I so selfish, so ungrateful, that I could not be trusted to work with her—for her—as she has done for me ?　Or am I something too fine and useless for working days ?"

"Why, my pet," I cried, "what unwonted mood is this you are in ? it is something new indeed, to see my little lassie captious. If I never spoke of those times, dear, it was certainly not because I regretted the mere worldly light of wealth and position that gilded them.　I was myself too young then, to set a high value on that.　The real sunshine that had faded from them, was of faithful, generous household affection.　I could not, even to you, bear to speak of my regrets for a loss that can never be repaired."

"And were you very rich and grand ?"

asked Miss Tresham, " had you horses and carriages, and a horse of your own to ride ? and did you go to many gay parties ? and——"

" Oh, stop, Laura, for pity's sake ! if you picture me to yourself, as having been quite a personage, I must disappoint you terribly, I fear. As the adopted daughter of the rector of a wealthy living, I had, of course, access to the best society the neighbourhood afforded—the society, that is, of families of culture and refinement. Sometimes I had even a glimpse into circles of higher rank and position than country clergy or untitled squires, but it was only a glimpse—that door was speedily barred against me." And I glanced at Jenny Colvin and exchanged a whole smile for her half one.

" And then you came, my lassie, a glad

surprise to our parents, a deep joy to me;
for you brought no slackening of the tie
that bound me to them. Rather they
seemed to redouble their watchful anxious
tenderness for me, as if they feared I might
fancy a change, though I never dreaded, or
suspected any. The living of Elmsley belonged to Mr. Wharnecliffe's father, and a
considerable fortune had devolved upon
him, at the death of a distant relative,
shortly after his second marriage. He had
expected no children from that marriage, as
your mother was past her youth and was
in delicate health, and they both agreed
that I should be their heiress."

Sybil lifted her head again.

" And then, I suppose, I came, and robbed
you of it all? Just like me ! I was born to
be a trouble to you !"

And down dropped the pretty head once
more.

" No, little maid, the loss you indirectly caused me, was even more yours than mine. Your dear mother never regained strength after your birth, she died when you were only a few months old, and left you, on her deathbed, a precious heritage to me. Her last act was to push towards me the baby that lay beside her, and with her last breath she whispered, ' May, her father and I have tried to make you forget that you were an orphan, do not let my baby miss her mother.' "

" And she never has !" cried Sybil, drawing fondly to her lips the hand that had lain caressingly on her hair. " You have been sister and mother both to her, always ! always !"

After a moment's pause, I continued—

" The fortune that Mr. Wharncliffe had inherited, was in the hands of a commercial firm, in which his relative had been a partner, and he had allowed it to remain there, partly from indolence, partly because he had been assured it was a profitable investment for it. After his second widowhood, he declared his intention of withdrawing the money, and closing his account with the firm, and he made a will, in which he divided the fortune equally between his own, and his adopted daughter. But he delayed too long. When you were only four years old, a report reached him that the firm had failed. He ordered his horse instantly, to ride to the nearest town, where the intelligence was confirmed. Whether his horse stumbled and threw him, or whether the shock he had received caused him to fall off insensible was never known, but the horse returned without its rider, and he was shortly afterwards discovered lying lifeless by the road-side. We were both orphaned, my Sybil, and as, secure in that luckless bequest, your father had neglected to make any other provision for us, we were penniless, except for a small sum for which my mother's life had been insured, and which was carefully invested for me when I should be of age."

"And all this sorrow," sighed my little sister, "you have had to bear alone!"

"But it is past and over now, girls," I answered cheerfully, "and we must not sadden our last evening together with sad recollections. Your father's friends came forward willingly to help me, and showed me the truest kindness in aiding me to help myself. Keeping a school seemed an arduous undertaking for a girl of one-and-twenty—a country girl, in London, too. But my education fitted me for the task; I

was promised a good connection,—and the
lease and furniture of this house was offered
me on very reasonable terms by the lady,
who wished to remove with her pupils to a
more fashionable locality, and my kind
friend, Miss Colvin, agreed to join me and
give me the very great advantage of her
practical good sense and experience." (Here
Jenny smiled a little gratified smile, and
made a slight movement of her head, as if
deprecating the compliment.) "And so we
struggled on for ten years,—losing some
friends, gaining others,—sometimes despon-
dent—oftener thankful and hopeful.

"And then came the change you know of.
An advertisement appeared in the papers,
enquiring for the grand-niece of Miss
Forbes, of Woodglen, Kelvydon, S—shire,
and promising something to her advantage.
I had long forgotten who and where were

my mother's distant connections,—who had
always ignored my existence,—but the advertisement caught the eye of an old friend
of ours who thought that it might be worth
attending to, and the charming result was,
that I awoke one fine morning, six months
ago, to find myself—to find myself and my
little sister—the owners of a nice little
country property, which devolved upon
me, as the nearest surviving descendant of
an aged spinster who had died without a
will, or without knowing, or seemingly
caring, who would succeed her in the possession of a fortune, which, if it does not
make us millionnaires, at least relieves me
from the necessity of working for a liveli-
hood, and enables me to gratify the wish
you have so long—and, apparently, hope-
lessly cherished—to leave London for green
fields and mountain scenery."

"Oh, the sweet old great-aunt!" cried Sybil,—"It was so beautiful of her to die without a will, and give her poor little niece a chance! Only think, Laura, a charming cottage in a picturesque country town, all among woods and hills! Just such a cottage as I used to admire in paintings, and think it would be heaven almost to live in! And now we have actually got one of our own!"

"It is very nice for you if you like it," replied her friend,—whose tastes, as the daughter of a Cornish county magnate, were more ambitious—"But it is quite a cottage ornée, I suppose?—Not a real cottage, like our lodge, for instance. They are very pretty to look at, but so full of rats and earwigs."

"Oh, as for that," said Sybil, "I am sure country earwigs are better than the black-beetles we have here ; but go on with your story, Mite."

"Why, child, my story is done—there is nothing more to tell."

The girls exchanged a look of blank disappointment, and Sybil burst forth indignantly,—

"Why, you are a regular cheat, Mite,—that is a mere sketch you have given us, and no story at all. I knew most of it before too. Surely, you don't call that keeping your promise ? You have told us nothing whatever about yourself ! "

"Nothing about myself? Whom else have I been talking about all this time ? What more did you expect to hear ?—and why do you look at each other so significantly, girls ? "

"We thought," — began Laura, and stopped short, glancing at Miss Colvin with a blush; but that little lady was busy counting the stitches in a crochet pattern, and did not look up.

Sybil spoke out audaciously,—" Laura thought, and I thought that you were going to tell us all your stories, all about your lovers."

Oh, to see Miss Colvin's face! The unfeigned horror and consternation in it moved me to a kind of sympathy, and checked the laugh which Sybil's remark had so nearly excited. So that I replied with becoming dignity, "Lovers? what do you know about lovers? young ladies who attend to their studies, have no time to think on such a subject."

"We know a great deal about them," rejoined my sister, saucily, glancing at the dismayed Lady Preceptress, "for Laura's sister Mary has had one for a year, and is going to be married to him in the autumn, and Laura is to be one bridesmaid, and I am to be another, if you'll let me, and you will, you darling, won't you? I said I would ask you to-day, because you can't refuse me on my birthday."

"We will talk about it later. I do not quite see how Laura can choose her sister's bridesmaids, or how you can take office under a bride you have never seen."

"No, no, Sybil, no more at present, it is late, march off to bed, both of you, you will be too much excited to sleep much to-night, and we must be stirring early, we have left many little things to do, yet."

"But, sister May," urged my lassie, "it is such a shame for you to put us off with such a meagre narrative, and call it the story of your life. Why, there is no life in it!"

"There seldom is much life in so much

of any story as we can *tell* of our own, my
pet. It is, as you say, a mere sketch."

"But the lovers! the lovers! the lovers!"
urged Sybil, with a vehement reiteration,
utterly regardless of the horror in Miss
Colvin's countenance, whose mouth twitched
convulsively, as with threatened paralysis,
at every repetition of the interdicted word.
But I was preceptress no longer, and
indulged myself in a laugh.

"Why, you little goose, what can I tell
you about lovers? where was I to find any?
Do you think lovers can be grown like
mushrooms in our dark old cellars here?"

"That is a foolish evasion, and deceives
nobody," answered Sybil, with an air of
grave rebuke. "No, Miette, we girls are
more observant and sagacious than you give
us credit for being. We know you have
had lovers, *passionate* lovers" (here Miss

Colvin emitted a groan,) "and we want to hear all about them."

"If," I laughed, "you can prove, from authentic sources, that I have had lovers, I promise to tell you all about them."

" There, Laura, you are witness she says she will tell us all about them. Well then, Miss Wharnecliffe, what about Captain Brereton, the widower father of the poor little girl who died (I can just remember her)—will you deny that he was a lover of yours ?"

"You have to prove that he was so."

"If not, why did he come here twice a week after school hours, to see you? why did he give you books and flowers? why did he——"

"Oh, nonsense, Sybil, you know poor little Fanny Brereton died in my arms; what was more natural, than that the father

of an only, an idolized child, should take a
melancholy pleasure in the society of one
who was so tenderly interested in her ?   If ·
he had not been a widower, this would have
excited no comment."

"May, I know you are very reticent.   I
shall begin to fear that you are very artful.
Now, blush for your equivocation.   Mrs.
Roscoe heard from Captain Brereton himself that you had refused him.   She told
her daughter Helen, who told Jane Purvis,
and so it became a tradition in the school,
which was handed down in whispers to our
time.   Ah ! see how she blushes, Laura."

"Well, since you know all about it, I
don't see why you should feel any curiosity
on the subject, but that you may not build
up any silly romance upon such a very common-place story, I'll tell you all about it.

"When little Fanny died, her father was so

touched by her affection for me, so grateful for my care of her during her illness, that he used to visit me occasionally in my leisure hours, to talk about her—to mourn for her. After a while he so far misunderstood my sympathy with his grief, so far overrated his own gratitude for that sympathy, as to —as to—"

" As to tell you he *adored* you ! And so he did ! Mrs. Roscoe said so, and that you were very unwise to refuse him ; why did you refuse him, Miette ?"

"Ah, why indeed! you who seem to think lovers are so plentiful ought to feel no surprise at that !"

" Oh, but he was young," Jane said, "and handsome, and rich, and so fond of you !"

Miss Colvin's forbearance was quite exhausted, and she gave audible expression to her disgust.

"Miss Wharnecliffe !—Sybil !—although I have no longer any authority over you you must allow me to say that your spirits quite overrun your discretion; your own maidenly delicacy ought to show you the impropriety of such conversation."

But saucy Sybil made a little jump at her, and catching her round the neck stopped the remonstrance with a kiss, crying, "It is my birthday, and I won't be scolded! I am sixteen, a woman grown, and not a school-girl any more. If you scold me I will make you tell us all about *your* lovers! I daresay you had plenty also, in your time!"

Laura Tresham looked dismayed at her friend's audacity, but the expected reproof came not. The "soft impeachment" of having had "lots of admirers" is one that a middle-aged maiden lady rarely resents.

Miss Colvin disengaged herself from her

accuser, merely saying, " I may or may not have had admirers, Sybil ; I was never so indelicate as to talk of them. Now, young ladies, bid good night, and retire."

The girls obeyed, but the incorrigible Sybil paused at the door.

" May, you are very heartless to laugh when Captain Brereton is named, you ought not to forget, that in his disappointment he exchanged into that regiment that went to the Crimea, and fell, bravely fighting at Balaclava. I wonder a woman can ever laugh who has lost a lover *so.*"

" Is that one of your school traditions, lassie ? Captain Brereton certainly went to the Crimea, because his regiment was ordered there, and not by exchange. I never heard of him again, but he is alive now, for all I know to the contrary. I am sure his name was never in the list of those who fell. Now, go, girls." And at last they vanished.

CHAPTER III.

IN INVISIBLE INK.

LEFT alone with Miss Colvin, I put up my feet on the fender stool, leaned back in my chair, and watched her proceedings. They were methodical, as her proceedings always were. First of all, she finished the row of crochet she had taken up, fixed the needle securely in the ball of wool, and deposited the whole in a little round basket at the back of her chair. Then she rose and moved noiselessly about the room, putting the books and ornaments away in the cabinet, covering what she did not remove from the dust with a dainty muslin coverlet. Then she pinned up the curtains, turned the hearth-rug face downwards, and having completed these thrifty arrangements, which she had never neglected for a single night during all the time she had presided over my little household, she sat down once more opposite to me, crossed her hands on her lap, and began slowly to rock herself up and down, a sure sign with her that she meditated conversation.

And then she broke silence, in the soft, whining tone, half fretful, half plaintive ; which yet, in the last ten years, had conveyed kindlier sympathy to my ears than I had heard in voices of more assumed sensibility.

Yet her opening address did not altogether please me.

"I am so glad, Miss Wharnecliffe" (nothing would ever induce Jane to call me by my Christian name); "so glad that you did not give your *whole* confidence to Sybil. To tell you the truth, I scarcely expected such reserve, but it was very wise of you—very."

"And why are you glad, Jane?"

One of Miss Colvin's peculiarities was that she never answered a direct question. She looked aside, smiled her little half-smile, and repeated—"It was so very wise. I always tell you that Sybil is sadly spoiled, and yet you have never given her a hint of your engagement to Mr. Challoner. I was afraid you would be tempted to break that discreet silence to-night."

"Well, I admit that I might have done so if Laura Tresham had not been present; and yet, no, I do not think I should have

yielded even then. My engagement to
Thorold has so long been a sacred secret
between us, that I am perfectly content
that it should remain so for the short time
that must yet elapse before he is free to
proclaim it to the world. I have never felt
the need of a confidante, and should certainly not seek one in a mere child like
Sybil. Why," I added, laughingly, "I
might forfeit all the dignified prestige of an
elderly maiden sister if she discovered that
I was looking forward to the close—in a
few months hence—of a sixteen years' romance! Is that what you meant when
you praised my wisdom, Jenny?"

"Sixteen years!" repeated Miss Colvin,
thoughtfully. "Dear me, how time flies,
to be sure—it does not seem so very long
since I came as your governess to Elmsley.
You, a tiny little thing of seven, whom

Master Thorold Challoner used to carry about in his arms, and lift up over his head to peep into the birds' nests or pull the peaches that were just a little too high for him to reach. What a great rough, domineering lad he was, and what a slave you were to him! How you used to creep out at his bidding, and follow him about like a wee dog. And when I complained to Mr. Wharnecliffe, he only laughed at me! He spoiled you as you spoil Sybil—dear me! And that is twenty-five years ago!"

"You were never Thorold's friend, Jane. I remember the solemn warning you gave my father, when you were leaving us, that I was too old (at fourteen) to run wild about the woods with a young man just going to the University."

"Yes, Miss Wharnecliffe, I did think so; and I was afraid that the fine head governess, who was engaged to 'finish' your education, might not be so observant of such *convenances* as I was. I was not much surprised when I heard, two years later, that you were affianced to Mr. Challoner. If I was surprised at all, it was that Mr. Wharnecliffe had still so much prudence as to wish to defer your marriage until you were of age. And to think that what seemed so prudent, should have been turned out so unfortunate! If you had married' at seventeen, it would have been with old Sir Edward's consent, and your fortune would have been settled upon you, and withdrawn from all danger of the subsequent wreck. Besides, what a different position both you and your sister would have been in all these years!"

"Well, well, they are past and gone. I shall never regret the trial, severe as it

has been, that has proved my Thorold's
faith so thoroughly."

"All's well that ends well, but it has
not ended yet ; and that is why I com-
mended you for not telling your sister of
your relations with Mr. Challoner, while
they are yet undefined and uncertain."

"Undefined and uncertain! You
ridiculous woman, they are neither—they
never have been either. When our engagement had existed for four years, with
Sir Edward's full approval, our 'relations'
were surely definite enough! When, on
the first tidings of my loss of fortune—and
in the first anguish of my orphanage, he
commanded his nephew to break it off, and
Thorold refused to violate his pledge to me
—refused me the right to absolve him from
it—our 'relations,' as you call them, remained unaltered, and neither undefined
nor uncertain."

"But so many years have passed since then; even now, another year must pass before your lover can return from New Zealand—in all those years you have never met—never even corresponded. Your engagement has been kept secret from your nearest friends—from Mr. Challoner's only brother. All these conditions Sir Edward imposed on his nephew; and he certainly believed, when he imposed them, that they would render your relations indefinite and uncertain."

"Very likely he believed so, but he was mistaken. He looked upon our attachment as a mere childish fancy, and could not think that any fidelity would stand so severe a test. I wish he had lived a little longer to see his error, and recant in due form."

"Still, Miss Wharnecliffe, you must not

be vexed with me for saying that there *is* an uncertainty in so very long an engagement, especially when absence and silence have made the parties to it almost strangers."

"Strangers! when we were playmates in childhood; when our mutual affection developed with our growth, as the summer fruit from the spring blossom? We know each other better than ever now, since we have learnt each other's unchangeable truth."

Still, Miss Colvin seemed hardly satisfied. "Twelve years!" she said; "it is a great piece out of a lifetime, and you might have married him then if he had accepted that appointment in Ceylon, instead of Sir Edward's New Zealand speculation. Have you never repented that?"

"Never for a moment; how could I

have gone with him to Ceylon, and left my little sister with strangers? You know all the physicians said that the climate would have been certain death to her."

"It was very good of you; few young women would have parted from a man whom they loved, as you loved Mr. Challoner, for the sake of a child who was after all no real kin to you."

"It was a simple duty; had she even been less dear to me, how could I have abandoned the child of those who had never suffered me to feel my own orphanage?"

"Still, I think you told me once that Mr. Challoner was not altogether pleased at the time, that you should have preferred your baby sister to him."

"Oh, Jane, you should not remember that against Thor. His displeasure—if there

was any—soon passed off. A baby of four
years old is a being of so little importance
in the eyes of a man who is not related to
her, that he cannot understand her conse-
quence in those of a woman. If Thor was
annoyed, it was at what he fancied was
the 'less' in my love for him, not the
'more' in my love for Sybil. He thought,
too, that I was sacrificing too much—"

Here I paused, but Jane rejoined—

"I know what you were going to say;
it would not offend me at all, my dear
Miss Wharncliffe. I am quite aware that
Mr. Challoner thought you were sacrificing
your social position in taking the duties of
a schoolmistress, and so, of course, in a
measure you were. It is very different
with me, I have been a governess nearly
all my life,—but for a lady, brought up as a
presumptive heiress, the affianced wife of Sir

Edward Challoner's nephew, and the sister-
in-law of the future Baronet of Hawkes-
hurst, it certainly was a derogation."

. "Well, well, that too is all over; when
Thorold comes next year to claim me he will
find me—if he cares for that—quite a lady
of property, dwelling on my own little
estate—how grand! But he will not be so
proud of that as I shall be of knowing that
he was ready and willing to claim me, let
my altered position have been what it
would."

"You may well be proud of his fidelity,"
said Miss Colvin, demurely; "I believe it
is not very common. I do not know much
about gentlemen myself—they have never
fallen much in my way—but I have always
heard that they are very inconstant. My
poor mother used to say they were like
eels, easy to catch, but hard to hold; that

any woman could *get* a lover, but not every
woman could *keep* one; and I do wonder
that you have always felt so satisfied of
Mr. Challoner's constancy, for I think,
until quite lately, you have never received
any greater assurance of it from himself
than was contained in that annual notice
from Sir Edward that he stipulated for
when he went to New Zealand."

"Nothing more than that—every year
on my birthday a line from old Sir Edward,
who was very punctual in his payment of
my annuity, though he took care never to
exceed the promised sum—'Mr. Thorold
Challoner is well, and desires his truest
love to Miss Wharnecliffe.' That was all.
It was enough. By my own true love I
knew what Thorold's was! Every year came
that line for ten years, then Sir Edward
died suddenly, and——"

Here my companion started from her
seat, alarm and horror on her countenance.
" Oh, good gracious ! I declare I have forgotten to wind up the school-room clock !"

" What does it signify ?" I asked, somewhat disgusted that my friend's attention
could wonder from my dearest interests to
such a trivial omission ; " you will be often
in the school-room before the clock will
have run down."

" But it is such a strange oversight !
Why I do not know that I ever once forgot
to wind that clock since you bought it ten
years ago ! Signify ? every little matter
signifies, especially in a school. You'll
excuse my leaving you ?—indeed it is late,
and I may as well bid you good-night."

And Jane, whose kind heart seldom
betrayed itself, in her undemonstrative manner stooped over me, and offered to my kiss

one cold, hard, passive cheek; then, seeming to think that our last evening together demanded a more cordial farewell, she came back as she reached the door, and offered me the other, which, from having been farther from the fire, was a little colder than the first; after which ceremony she glided noiselessly from the room.

I sat still for a little while after she left me, with my eyes fixed on the fire; then I roused myself with a laugh,—" A mere sketch," you said, my Sybil! and lo, as I sit musing here, the outline, filled in as it were with invisible ink, starts suddenly, at the magical touch of memory, into life and fulness! But it is not all invisible ink, I am happy to say, as I draw forth from my bosom my last, and almost my first, love-letter.

THOROLD CHALLONER TO MAY WHARNE-
CLIFFE.

" MY LITTLE MAYETTE,—

"When I sent you those few
hurried lines three months ago, the news
of my uncle's death was so recent, that I
could give you no details, simply because I
had received none. My brother, in communicating it to me, only said that it had
occurred rather unexpectedly a few days
before the mail started. I did not then
know that he had left me, as the saying is,
'provided for,' but I knew that in any
case I was now in a position to provide for
myself and for my good little wife also,
even if his sudden death had prevented
him from securing to me that long promised reward of my obedience to the hard
conditions he had imposed upon me. It

would have been hard, though, wouldn't it, if by any procrastination of his we had lost the reward, just as it was so nearly due to us ?

" But Sir Edward, if he has been harsh, has been honourable in this. He has bequeathed to me the whole of these broad acres to which he exiled me, and all the flocks and herds which have prospered in my charge, as in a second Jacob's. Then all the wealth, and it is considerable, that this land has produced since I have had the superintendence of it, he has carefully hoarded and profitably invested for me, and left it *in toto* to me without any reservation. So that I am actually a wealthier man than my elder brother Sir Franklin, and can give my bride gayer toilettes and purer diamonds than my haughty sister-in-law, Lady Harriet, can sport at the draw-

ing rooms! Is not that a triumph for a
feminine heart worth any waiting for,
Mayette? Can you not forgive uncle
Edward even our long separation, and my
enforced silence, for the sake of this magni-
ficent compensation?

"Well, rest his soul! I don't know that
we have so much to forgive, after all—certainly not from his point of view. I had
no right to expect from him more than a
younger brother's portion. Our marriage,
after poor Mr. Wharncliffe's ruin, would
have been a most improvident one, and I
owe him no grudge for compelling me to
earn the means of supporting a wife in the
rank my wife should hold.

"He was not wrong—of course I mean
from his point of view—in putting our
affection to even so severe a test as a twelve
years' absence. He had never much faith

in youthful constancy, and he knew that life in the Bush was most unfit for a girl brought up as you had been, while a love-correspondence would only serve to keep alive useless yearnings in a young man who had to work and not to dream.

" All has turned out for the best, as the goodies say. We are now within sight of the goal that seemed at such an illimitable distance when we parted. It has not been so very long after all, has it, dear ?

" By the bye, Sir Edward has affixed one condition to his bequest, not a legal condition, since it was stated only in a sealed letter left for me, but, of course, not the less binding on me. It was conveyed in a request that in the event of his dying before the expiration of the term of my exile, I would refrain from any announcement of our engagement until six months

after our meeting. This will not distress
you much, will it, my love? It need not
postpone our marriage, for the announcement of the one may serve for both.

"Perhaps he clung to a forlorn hope that
when we met we might quarrel? That
six months of intercourse might effect what
twelve years of separation had failed to do?

> "Like ships that have gone down at sea,
> When heaven was all tranquillity."

That, meeting and seeing the inevitable
change worked by the 'slow moving years,'
I might, which is very improbable, not like
you; or, which is much more likely, you
might not approve of *me!* 'Qui vivra
verra.'·

"And so my May is an heiress also, in a
small way? Fortune is prodigal of her
favours all at once. When I return home
I shall find my jewel in something more

like a becoming setting, than was that
formal, dingy old parlour, when I never
think of you but as seated with an awkward
squad of bread-and-butter misses around
you, a spelling-book in one hand, and a
birch rod in the other. Your little fortune
shall be settled on Sybil when we are
married, if you will, in proof that I have
forgiven you your preference of her to me
eleven years ago. Apropos of Sybil, I hope
you have brought her up with a proper
regard for my authority. I recollect that
she is my ward. When poor Mr. Wharnecliffe named me her guardian, he little
thought that my charge would be so purely
nominal. Can she remember me? She
was a pretty little trot—I hope she is good-
looking still, for I retain the infirmity with
which you used to reproach me, a positive
hostility to ugly women! If we had been

all these eleven years in Ceylon, you might have grown withered and yellow instead of being, as I am sure you still are, my delicate May-flower, my May queen, my fairy Miette ! You see I have forgotten none of the pet names I gave you when you were my little wife of seven years old, and which we shall neither of us have forgotten, I trust, when you are my little old wife of seventy !"

The letter dropped from my hand as I leaned back in my chair, musing, with a smile —and a sigh. The smile was at Thorold's imperious, masculine tone. So like him ! when, as Jenny reminded me, he used to tyrannise over me, in his domineering boyhood. Even as a lover he could not always, nor often, forego those airs of authority and rule. How he lays down the law that everything has been done for the best, and that

the sacrifice Sir Edward exacted from us was
but a trifling one after all! Time has passed
quickly with him in his active, laborious,
energetic life. And yet—eleven years of a
woman's youth is no light price to pay, even
for—Pshaw! was my sigh for those? What
matter though some of the bloom has faded.
I am my Thorold's May-flower still!

I gazed dreamily round the familiar apartment which he so uncivilly described as dingy
and formal (Jenny's state parlour too!) trying to recall my sensations when I first
entered it, a girl of one-and-twenty, snatched
so abruptly from youth's innocent pleasures
and sunny hopes to do battle with the
stern exigencies of toil and privation. I
remember how dreary the stiff dark room
had seemed to me, after the elegant luxury
of the Rectory, with its sunlight and flowers.
And how my poor little sister wailed and

pined at first, for the fresh, pure air, and the familiar faces. And how, as time crept slowly on (it had not flown fast with *me*, my Thorold! that room had become a sanctuary to me, from the memory of our last parting, a parting cheered by brave words of encouragement and promise, that had ever since been a cordial to my heart, nerving me to patient effort in the path, which only now, looking back on it, I saw to have been sad and lonely.

"Diamonds" indeed! as if I cared for jewels and fine toilets! More to me——

Here the wick of the lamp suddenly flared, and went out, leaving me in darkness. I rose, groped my way by the firelight to the hall table for my bedroom candle, and lighting it, stole softly up-stairs.

I had to pass through Sybil's room to mine, and I paused, as was my habit, for a

last glance at my sleeping treasure. She lay
as if asleep, but while I gazed on her beautiful
face, I saw two tears glitter on her long eye-
lashes, and trickle slowly down her cheek.
I knelt down by her bedside—" Sybil, my
pet ! is my lassie grieving to leave her old
home among her school-mates ?" But she
flung her arms round my neck, and sobbed
forth—

" Oh, May ! May ! I am nothing to you
but a dependent on your charity ! I have
no real sister !"

I soothed her with the fondest caresses,
and whispered tenderly, " My Sybil, if I am
ever less to you than I have been from your
birth, if I ever forget what I owe your
parents, or suffer the faintest shadow of
estrangement to come between us, then,
only *then*, cast it at me as a reproach—I
shall feel it as the bitterest—that I am 'not
your *real* sister !' "

CHAPTER IV.

ON THE PLATFORM.

THERE was no trace of tears on my young sister's blooming cheek, when she stood beside me on the railway platform the next morning, waiting till a few last words had been exchanged between Miss Colvin and me. Not even the parting, which, at a few stations further off, was to take place between her and her bosom friend Laura Tresham, could sadden her joyous exultation at the thought of "leaving school for good and going to live in the country." But then, warm-hearted and affectionate as Sybil was,

5—2

she had a healthy brightness of nature that refused to be clouded by any merely sentimental sorrow. She had been, from almost infancy, the pet and plaything of her schoolfellows, and was accustomed to the inevitable separation from one after another, as they left my care to return to their parents' homes. These partings had not for her the melancholy significance that parting has for those whose family circle has such a character of permanence, that any breach in it is like the displacement of a stone in a cloister wall, giving a sense of insecurity by the very glimpse it offers of the changing world without. Rather, to my lassie these disturbances were like the breeze rippling a quiet lake, displacing for a moment the landscape mirrored on its waters, but passing over it, to leave it unbroken as before.

Besides, had not Laura promised to be

our first visitor, when we should be quietly
settled at Woodglen? Had not Sybil
already fixed on the room she would select
for her friend, in her imaginary picture of
the cottage she had never seen? Not the
very best room, that was to be kept for Miss
Colvin, who had also engaged to visit us
during her six weeks' holidays at Midsummer. And the next best is for the lady
of the house, "a ridiculous little person"
(so Sybil said), "who could never be pre-
vailed on to appropriate the best of anything;
but the next best she *shall* have." Sybil
will have the little room next to hers, and
Laura's shall be that from which her friend's
opens as a dressing-room, "or if it does not
May will alter it so that it shall, for it is
our very own house, to do what we like with,
you know, Laura dear!"

Here a fat German, who had just de-

scended from an up-train, hurrying along
the platform with a carpet-bag, as heavy as
himself, swung ruthlessly against Sybil, who
caught Laura's arm, with a faint scream.
The German muttered an impatient oath,
and was hastening on, when his glance rested
on the lovely face, turned upbraidingly upon
him. He stopped instantly, took off his hat,
and offered an abject apology.

This little interlude over, while the girls
laughed and whispered their comments upon
it, I resumed my conversation with Jane,
who stood holding a bird-cage, covered with
a silk handkerchief, her parting gift to my
sister, and looking, now that our last parting was so imminent, just a shade fluttered
and anxious. Yet she repelled my sympathy with her, on the dulness of returning
to an empty house.

"Dull, dear Miss Wharnecliffe? well, it

may be so just at first, but I shall have no time to be dull, I have so much to do. You'll write to me this week, won't you? And about Mr. Coates; you do not advise me to change, not yet? as Laura is leaving, perhaps his teaching will be advanced enough for the young ladies who return after these Easter holidays. They are so much younger."

" Take your seats, ladies, take your seats ! ring-a-ting, ring-a-ting."

Here followed the usual hearty embraces, and scrambling up into the carriages as the train engine's admonitory puff was heard. Sybil took the canary from her friend, who stood on tip-toe to call out " Good-bye, *au revoir !* Take care, Sybil, there is water in the cage ; oh, dear, you have spilled it all over me !"

And my last vision of Miss Colvin for that time was of a distressed countenance, anxiously bent over her silk dress, from which she was wiping the drops that had fallen on it from the cage ; all the drops that fell on either side.

When Laura changed her train at Reading, there followed, of course, a "da capo" of kisses and farewells, and Sybil leaned from the window, as long as the figure on the platform was visible, to wave her adieux to her ; but when she drew in her head again, the smiles sparkled gay as ever on her rosy dimpled mouth. Decidedly, my lassie is not senti-mental.

Our fellow passengers got out at Reading too, and when we sped on, my sister and I had the carriage to ourselves, which I was glad of, as I availed myself of the opportunity to ask her—

" By the way, my child, what was that you were telling me last night—that Mary Tresham was going to be married ?"

"Yes," answered Sybil gleefully, "she is going to be married to her cousin, to whom she has been attached for years, Laura says."

"Not for many years I should think, for Miss Tresham cannot be much older than Laura?"

"Laura is seventeen, sister May, and Mary is nineteen, and she has been fond of her cousin ever since they were children."

"I remember seeing Mary once, when her aunt, who was an old acquaintance of your mother's, was in town. They had come up to consult Dr. Halford about Mary's lungs, they feared she was consumptive, she certainly looked very delicate."

"So she was, so she is," replied Sybil, "and they took her to Italy last winter, where her cousin joined her, and they became en-

gaged. She is ever so much better now, it
was all on the nerves, Laura says, and she
will get well, now that she is so happy, and
they are to be married in the autumn."

"And what is the cousin's name?"

"His name? Really I don't know. Laura
always calls him Cousin Willy, and she says
Mary is so fond of him; before they were
engaged she used to treasure up the bou-
quets he gave her, and kiss even his hand-
writing in his little notes to her father or
herself."

"Little notes? Then they lived near
each other?"

"His estate adjoined Mr. Tresham's; he
is very rich. Mr. and Mrs. Tresham were
always anxious that he should marry Mary,
and they are all so glad!"

I thought of the pale girl, on whose
fragile form the seeds of fatal disease had

been so plainly set, and sighed as I pictured her to myself stretching forth weak hands to grasp the flower of youthful life, so surely to drop from their dying hold. Sybil understood my sigh.

"I tell you, Mite," she repeated, "that Mary is getting quite well; she will be well in the autumn, the doctors say, and meantime she is too happy to keep on being ill!"

"Then you think happiness must be a cure for illness, pet, and 'that going to be married' is the highest point of felicity?"

"No, I don't," answered the little maiden, somewhat offended; "that is—Laura says it is, but I—I am not quite sure, I reserve my opinion. For the present I can imagine no greater happiness than this of having my sweet sister May all to myself for evermore, flying along the line in an express train (do

put up your window, my lap is full of blacks)
on our way to a beautiful country home, all
green fields, and birds and flowers. Dicky-
bird, dicky-bird, aren't you glad! Look
there, Mite, there's a beautiful cottage! is
ours like that?"

"I only saw it once, in the depth of winter
—it will be almost as new to me as to you,
dear; but, Sybil, don't chatter so. We
have several hours of travelling yet before
us, and I am tired already."

" So you are—you look quite pale. The
fact is, sister, you require to be fed, and lo!
I am going to feed you. Behold the manna
wherewith Miss Colvin thoughtfully provided me."

So saying, Sybil produced from a basket
a packet of sandwiches, which she unfolded
before my yearning eyes, and laid on the
seat fronting her, while she searched in her

basket for a little phial of wine which she proceeded to pour into a wine-glass without a foot.

But, alas! "there is many a slip 'twixt the cup and the lip,"—a sudden jolt, as the carriage drew up at a station, sent the contents of the glass into my bosom, and as I was drying it, a stout woman, heated and panting with the weight of a fat baby of some ten months old, rushed up to the opened door and hastily deposited the infant on the sandwiches! My companion and I exchanged a look of dismay; but the train was overdue — the platform was crowded with expectant passengers. The mother was hurriedly receiving baskets and parcels from friends outside, heedless of the cries of the baby, who seemed to find our destined repast an uncomfortable seat (perhaps owing to the mustard). At last,

Sybil mildly addressed her. " Please take him up ; he's sitting on our sandwiches."

" On your sandwiches ?" repeated the outraged parent, snatching him up with the abruptness that seemed to characterise all her movements,—" Oh ! *poor dear little fellow !*"

Less than this would have provoked a school-girl's laughter, and Sybil burst forth into such a peal of merry music that it attracted the attention of a gentleman who was hurrying along the platform, looking for a vacant seat. Just at that moment, our companion made the discovery that she was in the wrong class. Out she tumbled, with all her belongings, and the gentleman entered our carriage, and took the seat opposite to me, only just escaping the desecrated dainties which, to my horror, Sybil regardlessly tossed out of the door.

I was so scandalised at such an indecorum, that, to mark my disapproval, I turned away from her to devote my attention to a book I had brought with me, and never raised my eyes, until, at the next station, my *vis-à-vis* got out, and went across the line, to speak to some acquaintance he saw there.

"That's an officer," remarked Sybil,— "he has been wounded in some war; did you see that his left sleeve was empty?"

"I did not observe it. I never stare at strangers."

"And"—continued Lassie, quite heedless of the implied rebuke,—"he's a Colonel Somebody."

"Now, Sybil, how *can* you tell that?"

"I saw it on the little box he popped under the seat, before I could read the name. I'll fish it out."

"Sybil! I order you to sit still! How can you be so unlady-like?"

"What a lovely beard this colonel has! It is like gold floss silk! And what a—"

Here the giddy child's observations were silenced by the re-appearance of the wearer of the "lovely beard," who resumed his seat. But Sybil was too excited to remain quiet, and presently began to twitter and chirp to her bird, forgetful of Miss Colvin's dictum, that it was highly improper for a lady to move or speak in a railway carriage. I looked up to reprove her, and met the eyes of our fellow traveller fixed so intently on me that, slightly confused, I looked down on my book again. If it had been my young sister he was staring at!—

Still conscious of his fixed gaze, I looked up again. Yes, he was still watching me;

but this time there was a smile on his lips,
—and then came the sudden mutual recognition.

" Miss Wharnecliffe ! "

" Captain Brereton ! "

And at the moment of our cordial
greeting, Sybil ceased to talk to her canary,
and looked on with amazement and interest.

Colonel Brereton turned to her and held
out his hand.

" And this is Sybil,—the little girl I saw
nine years ago in short frocks and long
curls ? She was then not much younger
than my poor Fanny,—the rose-bud has
nearly bloomed into a rose, and the rose
itself—"

" Has faded so much," I laughed, " that
you did not recognise it ! Mistook it, perhaps, for a poppy ? "

VOL. I.   6

"True, I did not immediately recognise
you," he answered, "because you were so
silent and grave. Your voice and smile
would at once have betrayed you. But to
what happy chance do I owe this meeting?
I have heard nothing of you since you
banished me so inexorably from Bedford
Square. Tell me,—is Miss Colvin there
still? Does the establishment still pros-
per?"

"You can have heard nothing of me
lately, or you would know that the establishment, as you call it, is now wholly
resigned to Miss Colvin's government,—that
an old lady has died without a will in
Kelvydon, in S—shire, that I, as a descendant of her family, have succeeded to her
modest possessions,—and Sybil and I are
now on our way to install ourselves in our
new home."

" At Kelvydon! You are going to Kelvydon? I am going to Plaistow Manor, which is only six miles from Kelvydon. Admiral Stacy, of Plaistow Manor, is a cousin of mine, and I have my head-quarters there, while the builders are pulling to pieces my own place in Somerset-shire."

Here Sybil joined in eagerly.

"If you know Kelvydon, Colonel Brereton, do tell us something about it. Is it pleasant there? Do nice people live there? Is Woodglen very pretty?"

" You will soon be able to judge of some of those points for yourself," he answered smiling, " for here we are at Folbridge, where we wait an hour for the Kelvydon train. You will have only an hour's ride before you when we start again. And so you inherit from old Miss Forbes of Woodglen? I heard, when I was last at the Stacys', that the lawyers were advertising for her next-of-kin; but I never dreamt of meeting in the heiress my long-lost friend."

Here we were interrupted by the necessity of alighting at the junction. Having repaired the loss of our sandwiches in the refreshment-room, I left Sybil in the waiting-room, occupied in ministering to the comforts of her canary, while I accepted Colonel Brereton's proposal to take a turn with him on the platform. I was very glad to have him with me. The first excitement of the start was over, re-action had already set in, and, travelling through a strange country to a strange home, I felt quite the "unprotected female," and the presence of a masculine companion seemed to give me confidence and courage.

Nor was my satisfaction at all alloyed by any embarrassing recollection that we had " parted in silence and tears," nine years ago, when he had honoured me with the offer of his hand,—declined (it is no disloyalty to Thorold to avow it) with a tender regret,—not a regret that I could not accept his love, but that the assurance of my regard should seem such a *banalité*,—since I could not tell him my secret, nor why his suit was hopeless.

I wondered, had he forgotten all that? He was much changed, and the change was not for the worse. He was graceful, intelligent, and distinguished looking, then, as now, but he had lost that expression of melancholy, and almost morbid sensibility which, in earlier days, had made him seem rather—well, not exactly effeminate, but less manly than he was now, when there

was enough of worldly *aplomb* and
masculine dignity about him to give to the
courteous gentleness of his manner, that
almost imperceptible touch of condescension,
that has for a woman the charm of a subtle
flattery.

In old times, I had looked down on him,
I am afraid a woman always does look down
a little on the man whose passion for her
she does not return ; but he seemed altogether superior to me now.

"And so you are going to live at Woodglen ?" he resumed, as we paced the railway
platform together, not a very romantic
promenade certainly, yet one that has perhaps been the scene of more tender or pathetic
incident than many a sylvan shade. "For
you who never took kindly to city life, the
change will doubtless be pleasant, but how
will it suit your bright little sister ? "

"Oh !" I answered, "it is even a greater happiness to Sybil than to me, to leave town, she has always so longed for green fields, always so enjoyed a holiday among them, whenever I could afford to give her one. You know, in town or country, a school-girl's life must be monotonous, and until quite lately, I could not give her even such pleasures as are accessible to very modest purses in London."

"She does not seem to have pined for them, she is very bright, and singularly lovely !"

"You think so ?—I am so glad, — of course I think her perfect, but I like to find my judgment confirmed by more impartial observers."

"Nay," said my companion, smiling, "I did not go so far as to say she was perfect. Every man has his own standard of perfec-

tion.   Sybil needs some years of maturity
to be measured by *mine.*"

"Her girlish beauty I do think perfect,
but of course her character is as yet imma-
ture, as a school-girl's must be.   And Sybil
is a mere school-girl! affectionate and
impulsive, with as yet no thought beyond
the narrow sphere of schoolroom discipline,
and schoolmates' attachments."

"As for the discipline," remarked Colonel
Brereton slily, "that packet of sandwiches,
which she flung into my face——"

"Ah, you must not judge her by her
behaviour to-day; a young girl may be
pemitted to be a little excited by the joy
of leaving school for good.   And whatever
else Woodglen may be, it will be my little
sister's first real home.   As such I am sure
she will like it."

"There is no fear that she will not like

it, if her tastes are as rural as you say they are. Woodglen is a very pretty place, and Kelvydon is in a charming country. I know it well, having been in the habit of visiting in the neighbourhood from my boyhood."

"Did you know Miss Forbes ?"

"I did not. She was very old and infirm, and I believe, had been confined to her room for years. I don't think any one of the present generation knew much of her, unless perhaps my old friend Miss Hogge, who knows everybody."

"And now, leave my affairs," I said, "and tell me about yourself. Why have we been so long without meeting ? and even now, our meeting is accidental."

"You remember," he replied, "that when I placed my little girl in your charge, I told you, that when I lost her mother I left my house, and let it for a term of years, until, as I hoped, my Fanny's education should be completed."

"Yes, I know, but you have not gone back there, yet."

"No, I accompanied my regiment to Sebastopol, where I received a colonelcy in exchange for an arm. Not a bargain to please any lady, I fear."

"I don't know about that. The Crimean war was a long time ago,—where have you been since?"

"I received other wounds, beside that in my arm, and the medical men advised a milder climate for me than England, in which to regain my health. So I travelled in Syria, and Spain, until a few months back, when my home in Somersetshire came into my own possession again, and it is now being improved, added to, and re-built, for my final occupation."

" You speak in the singular number, you are not married, then ?"

" Do you know, Miss Wharnecliffe, I am surprised that you have so long delayed to put that lady's query ! I am rather hurt that you should seem to have thought it a superfluous one to a poor old maimed soldier like me."

" What affectation, Colonel Brereton ! as if you did not know well, that a mutilation, suffered in honourable warfare, will heighten the interest any woman can feel for a brave man."

" Do *you* think so ? really ?"

I looked up in his face, a little startled by his sudden change of tone, then something in his eyes made me drop my own, with—I felt it—a deep blush.

A silence ensued which was broken by the blessed whistle of the railway engine.

I hastened to call Sybil, and presently we were again in motion. The carriage was nearly full, and Colonel Brereton had some difficulty in finding himself a seat. He left the train at the next station, and bade us adieu, promising to come and see us when we should be settled at the cottage. But it was my sister, and not I, who pressed him to do so.

CHAPTER V.

WOODGLEN.

IF Woodglen had proved far less attractive than it really was, I do not think that either Sybil or I was in a mood to feel any dissatisfaction with it. But far more captious critics than we were, would have found nothing to blame. Kelvydon itself, although it laid claim to the dignity of a market town, and asserted its claim, architecturally, by a stately town hall in which were public rooms for balls and concerts,—a market place,—a "restored" church,—and a modern hotel, "limited," both as regarded its liabilities and its accommodation,—Kelvydon, with all this magnificence, occupied less space than many a suburban village, and like a man whose house is too large for his means, had often to struggle hard for the cash, whether collected as voluntary subscriptions or parochial rates, necessary to maintain this splendour.

It was a neat little town, built on the side of a lofty hill, around which were grouped other hills, still more lofty, commanding on every side charming views of woods, and sunny slopes, and commons, golden with gorse already, and soon to be purple with heather. In the green valley at its foot, flowed a gleaming river, a mere rivulet as to width, but then everything in Kelvydon was on a small scale. The very hills—lofty as hills—were, in fact, miniature mountains, and the brook made as much fuss, as it brawled and prattled along its stony bed, as if it had been the father of waters itself, and as if the sea were waiting for it, though it was merely a tributary to a larger river that received it ten miles further off.

Woodglen was situated at the bottom of the street that climbed the hill, only fenced from it by iron rails round a little garden court ; but the cottage itself was quite a cottage *ornée.* The court was planted with costly shrubs of many years' growth—roses, jessamine, and wistaria were trained up to the very roof—and when you crossed the pretty vestibule to the drawing-rooms behind, you might fancy yourself in a rural seclusion, miles away from such vulgar realities as public-houses and butchers' shops.

The neighbours' "backs" were well planted

out with screens of evergreen shrubs and
trees. The church alone was full in view,
and the rectory, on higher ground just
outside the town, looked down upon us
with a friendly, patronising air. The
drawing-room windows opened on a lovely
lawn and garden, bounded only by the
laughing river, across which a rustic bridge
led to a woodland path winding round a
hill clothed with plantations of oak and
fir, and wearing on its summit a space of
table-land, on which the rays of the early
spring-time glittered like a crown.

Sybil's raptures were irrepressible—she
danced up and downstairs, she raced from
room to room, she peeped into every closet
and cupboard, she overwhelmed me with
embraces, welcoming me to our new home,
congratulating herself and me on the discovery of every fresh attraction, and only

calmed down when the gathering twilight
compelled me to forbid her any further
sallies into the garden, and to order her
to expend her superabundant activity in
unpacking my boxes, and arranging my
bedroom in preparation for an early retreat.

When I rose the next morning, I felt
enough of the fatigue of the past journey
to be glad of the excuse of a pouring wet
day for keeping my sister within doors, and
employing her in some of the thousand-
and-one little domestic offices implied in
the word "settling," while I sat down to
the late Miss Forbes' rather antique writ-
ing-table to announce our safe arrival to
dear old Jenny Colvin.

I did that first as a matter of duty, and
then I proceeded to indite a second letter
for my own pleasure, but not for mine

only—a long letter, minutely descriptive, sometimes narrative, sometimes retrospective—a letter to one far, far away, who had been toiling there for years to make all that could now be a home to me—the home that we should share together. Now and then I would pause, and look up with a smile to listen to Sybil's bird-like notes, as she gaily carolled over-head.

Little puss! she calls this her home "for ever." She little dreams that after all it is only a very brief tenancy she will enjoy of it. That in a year—in a year and a half at most—she will be whisked away to some distant county to grace her new brother's mansion with the sweet girlish loveliness that his poor little faded wife cannot bring him.

Yes, I rejoiced that Lassie was pretty. Thorold had always a passion for beauty, and

since our young sister must live with us
until she finds a home of her own, I was
glad that his taste would not be wounded
by awkward movements or an unsightly
face. To bring Sybil into his house will,
be like hanging some exquisite painting
on his walls, to be an unfailing source of
pleasure to him. For me —— all *my*
charm must be in the fond fidelity that
takes no note of change; and I am far
prouder of this than of any homage to mere
beauty, which I could claim from other
men as well as from him.

Something like this was on my pen,
when it was suddenly twitched out of my
hand, and before I could remonstrate, the
paper itself as abruptly disappeared, and
a gay voice laughed mischievously at my
ear.

" Not another line, May ; you have been

7—2

writing too long already. Here, I see, is
a letter to Miss Colvin ; that shall go, but
as for these long, closely written pages—
no, don't snatch, I am not trying to read
it—I know, by the length of it, that it is
to my guardian, Mr. Challoner; the mail
does not start till Friday, so you have
heaps of time; put it away and talk to
me. You are my governess no longer, remember, but my companion only. I won't
be neglected in this shameful way, for an
old fogy you have not seen for ages. If it
was that dear Colonel Brereton now,
with his elegant figure, and his soft blue
eyes—!"

"Oh, Sybil!" I remonstrated, "you are
positively vulgar. How can you talk of
men as if you were a servant girl? I fear
your companions hitherto have been ill-
chosen, if this is a specimen of the talk—I

cannot call it conversation—you have been accustomed to with them. As for your preference of Colonel Brereton to your guardian, I am sorry you are so easily won by new faces from old friendships."

" Old friendships! Why, I never saw Mr. Challoner since I was a mere baby, and he has forgotten me, and never sends me a message even. And I do not see why you should trouble yourself to write those long business letters, now that you are rich, and can do without his advice, which is all, I suppose, that you write to him for. Why do you laugh, Miette ?"

" I laugh at your foolishness, child; you know well, or ought to know, that your guardian is my oldest, dearest, truest friend. He will be here, I hope, in the course of the summer, and I shall be much

disappointed if, when you know him,
you do not love him a thousand times
more than the first slight acquaintance
you chance to meet in a railway carriage."

Sybil tossed her shining head, and fixed
her eyes on mine with an air of grave reproof.

"May, I have a great mind not to be a
woman yet!"

"No danger, my love; you are
the merest baby I ever saw of your
inches."

"Because," she continued, without noticing my remark, "I begin to see by you
that to be a woman is to be cold, and hard,
and ungrateful for the love that was
lavished on you in your girlhood, not so
very long ago."

"Mercy on us, what a tirade! When

have you seen such evil-mindedness in poor harmless me ? "

"You know you acknowledged that Colonel Brereton had been the lover of your youth, yet you are so indifferent now to that remembrance, that you talk to him as coolly as if you were his grandmother, and you can call a being who has never come near you since you were no older than I am, your dearest and truest friend."

" Sybil, I will have no more of this nonsense, you do not know what you are talking about. I am not forgetful of 'the lover of my youth'—oh, God forbid !—nor ungrateful to him, and you will know this when you understand such subjects better. Go now and bring down my books for this empty bookcase; but first, give me back my letter."

She obeyed, and ran off, singing gaily

as before. Silly child! She and Laura Tresham will be inventing some wonderful romance I should not wonder, of which the maimed Colonel will be the hero.

CHAPTER VI.

A FIGURE OF FUN.

WE had been more than a week at Woodglen, and were beginning to feel it more homelike, though with familiarity with the locale, came a sense of isolation at being still strangers among our townsmen. Sybil was disappointed that no one as yet had wished to seek our acquaintance, and was scarcely consoled by the suggestion of old Bessie, our predecessor's confidential servant, whom I had inherited with the property, that "the spring fashions wouldn't be out until next

week, and may be the Kelvydon ladies were
waiting for their new bonnets!" She further
informed us that the rector was old and
very infirm, and never went out; that the
gentleman who preached for him last Sun-
day was a stranger, the curate, Mr. Mervyn,
being absent on a visit to his friends in
Dorsetshire, and that the doctor's lady was
"laid up" with her eighth baby, and—and
she did not think there were any more, the
likes of us, in Kelvydon.

Truly our social prospects did not look
very bright!

It rained too almost incessantly, and all
these unfavourable circumstances, with the
reaction from her previous excitement, began
to tell, even on my gay-hearted Lassie, and she
was looking as forlorn as she ever did look,
as she stood one morning at the window of
the breakfast-room, gazing wistfully into the

street, trying to persuade herself and me that the leaden sky was clearing, and that it would be safe to lay aside my work and prepare to accompany her in a ramble through the dripping, and still leafless woods.

Suddenly she uttered an exclamation.

" Oh, May ! Do come here and look ! Such a figure of fun ! with such a bonnet ! and pattens ! and—oh, good gracious ! she's nodding to me ! She is coming to the house !"

A sharp peal at the door-bell confirmed this statement, and in another moment there was a suppressed whispering in the vestibule—a clatter of pattens on the oil-cloth, a flapping of a wet umbrella, and then the parlour maid entered and announced " Miss Hogge," followed into our astonished presence by a visitor whose appearance certainly justified Sybil's epithet of a "figure of fun."

Her dress was of a fashion obsolete in the memory of my generation, and of a taste which it is to be hoped, for the credit of our ancestresses, was never in vogue at any time, though the materials were rich, and had once been costly. In describing it, I describe Miss Hogge's invariable costume, on what she called "state occasions," at least it never varied while I knew her, nor in the memory of any one in Kelvydon.

It consisted of a black satin dress, very short and very scanty (we were then in the days of trains and crinoline), trimmed from top to bottom with little frills, sleeves that were too tight and too short for her, supplemented with long scarlet worsted mittens, a gaily embroidered crape scarf and a black beaver bonnet, surmounted by a plume of feathers that might have served for a hearse.

But strange as was this toilet, my attention soon wandered from it to become riveted on the wearer. She was a woman of about sixty, of middle height, and slightly marked with small-pox. Her forehead was low, her nose retroussé, her mouth large and coarse, though embellished with even rows of strong white teeth, of which she was no niggard in display.

Not a prepossessing face, yet at the first glance I was attracted, and could not look away from the wonderful eyes that lighted it. Large full eyes, very large; very bright, very black; with a heavy fringe of raven lashes, and eyebrows finely arched, and delicately pencilled—the only trait of delicacy in a countenance that expressed power but no refinement. Eyes that glittered with humour—that blazed with passion—that glanced with keen penetration, from which nothing could escape, but yet from whose depths looked forth an unutterable pathos, as of a chained soul mutely questioning other souls "what of the night?" in which all were wandering.

Not that I understood the pathetic look then, but I was intuitively conscious of it from the moment I met those eyes, and it made me at once regardless of the ridiculous or grotesque in the attire of my new guest, as I went forward to greet her.

"Miss Wharnecliffe? May Wharnecliffe?" she said in a not unmusical voice, though with something of a lisp in it, and glancing keenly at Sybil, who had withdrawn to the window to hide her mirth.

"I am Henny Hogge, my dear. My father came here forty years ago, and I have lived here ever since. I wanted to be the first to

welcome you to Kelvydon, and I hope I am,
for in this wet weather I am sure no one
will come out in her best clothes, and no
Kelvydon lady will pay a first call in
other than *grande tenue.* You are wondering why *I* came out in my best? (detecting,
to Sybil's confusion, the glance she threw
at our visitor from her retreat) but *my* best
things were made when things were meant
to last, which they never are now, and
besides, I have got an umbrella as big as a
tent, and a little rain won't hurt me! So,"
she continued, seating herself beside me,
without further noticing Sybil—" so I am
the first? Well, I'm glad of that. I would
have come sooner, but I only got Johnnie's
letter yesterday, telling me that his old
friend had come to Woodglen? You know
that Johnnie Brereton is also an old friend
of mine ?"

I assented.

"Yes, I have known Johnnie since he was a boy at Chailey grammar school, when my brother was head master there; I know all about Johnnie, and through him, all about you."

"You can know but little of me, through Colonel Brereton?" I smiled, "for until we met accidentally the other day, we have held no communication for years."

"I know that too, but it makes no difference—a portrait, thoroughly well painted, is a likeness for ever. Besides, you have been kept out of the glare of the world, and so—who is that girl? I don't know her."

"That is my sister Sybil—Colonel Brereton must have spoken to you of her?"

"If he had, I should not have forgotten— I never forget—Sybil, do you call her? Come here, my dear, and let me look at you."

But, peremptory as was the command, Sybil found it impossible to obey. Miss Hogge's oddities had been too much for her limited stock of decorum, and she was writhing with suppressed laughter. Quick as was the reproving glance I shot at her, Miss Hogge's was quicker still to detect it, but she only smiled, showing all her white teeth, rather wolfishly, while she said in a soft coaxing tone (I found out later, that she always spoke her bitterest things in her softest voice)—

"She is laughing at old Henny, the darling! It is the nature of young girls to titter. They are always merry at the bread-and-butter and pinafore age."

Fancy Lassie's disgust! She was grave in a moment, and came forward with an attempt at dignified self-possession, which was more laughable than Miss Hogge's

peculiarities. That lady looked scrutiniz-
ingly at her, until the girl's fair face flushed
with mingled bashfulness and displeasure;
then her tormentor turned to me—

"She is not a bit like you—no one would
take you for sisters—she——"

But when she looked round again Sybil
had escaped from the room.

"Ah, she is gone! What a beautiful
creature she is! Why, my dear, you will
be the envy and grudge of all the mothers
of grown-up daughters in the county!
All our young men will go wild about
her."

"Sybil is certainly beautiful," I answered.
"I wonder Colonel Brereton did not tell
you that."

"I don't wonder that Johnnie never
thought about her," replied my visitor significantly, so significantly that I was silly

enough to blush, and said, to hide my confusion,—

"And she is as innocent as she is lovely.
Please do not talk before her of the admiration she will excite : she does not care
for it, as yet, and I am not anxious to fore-
stal the time when she will claim it."

"Ah, I see," said Miss Hogge, with a
slight sneer, which she immediately tried
to conceal with the blandest smile ; "you
would put your dial in the shade, and persuade yourself the sun has not dawned !
Well, she does look very much as if she
had been reared among the violets ; but
never mind her, it is you whom Johnnie
told me to come and see."

And certainly Miss Hogge obeyed her
friend's directions to the letter, for she fixed
her bold black eyes on mine, and stared at
me so persistently, that I began to feel like

8—2

a mesmeric patient beneath the gaze of a
"medium."

"Do you like Johnnie Brereton, Miss
Wharnecliffe ?"

"Indeed I do, or rather I did ; but it is
so long since we parted, only to meet for a
few hours in travelling, and he may have
altered very much since we were friends.
He has altered very much externally."

"Not that I can see. He has lost an
arm and grows a great beard—he is more a
man of the world than he was—I like him
better as he is—I wonder will you ?"

"You must give me time to decide on
that point," I replied, laughing ; "perhaps I
shall have no opportunity. Colonel Brereton does not live near Kelvydon."

"No, but he is very often here, at his
cousin's, Admiral Stacy, of Plaistow Manor,
and you are sure to meet him there, even

if you are too prudish to receive gentlemen
visitors at Woodglen."

"But I do not know the Stacys."

"You will know them soon : Mrs. Stacy
is sure to call—indeed Johnnie writes me
word that he is going to bring her here the
first fine day."

"Very kind of Colonel Brereton, and
very kind of Mrs. Stacy; is she—?"

"Nice?" suggested my visitor, as I
paused. "Well, no, I think her uncommonly nasty."

(Oh, if Miss Colvin had heard that speech
her hair would have stood on end.)

"I can't bear Mrs. Stacy," continued the
outspoken lady, "and she can't bear me.
But it does not follow that you will not
think her nice, when she comes here, all
smiles and suavity, to do the gracious grand
lady to the humble little one; but just

wait till your pretty sister has attracted some *bon parti* whom Madam Stacy has destined for one of her own daughters, see if she will not sharpen her claws and bite your back then, for she never flies at the face."

I began to feel glad that Sybil had vanished, and to wonder whether the theory of counterparts would account for the refined Colonel Brereton's choice of a female friend ! Those magical eyes seemed to read my thought.

" You think me a spiteful old maid, don't you ?" she said ; " but there is an old quarrel between Mrs. Stacy and me—I will tell you all about it some day, for you and I must be friends, May Wharnecliffe. I like you—I liked your portrait, as Johnnie sketched it for me, ten years ago—I like the original better still."

"Was it a faithful portrait ?" I asked, rather glad to escape from the topic of Mrs. Stacy's shortcomings, for Miss Hogge's eyes had gleamed with almost ferocity while she spoke of them.

"Yes," she replied, still staring fixedly at me; "it is still faithful, thanks to that slight, mignonne figure. At your age, my dear, your sister will be twice your girth— and those delicate, sensitive features. It is not such a man as our friend Johnnie who would be tempted to look away from it, by the mere girlish bloom and freshness of —Sybil, do you call her ? but there is one very odd thing about you, May Wharne-cliffe."

There are a great many odd things about you, Henny Hogge, thought I, but I only said,

"What is it ?"

"It is an expression of serenity, of calm
—the peace, not of hope, nor of patience,
but of attainment."

"And you find that strange ?"

"Yes, in a woman of your age, and of
your experience. Johnnie has told me
something of it. You are yet too young
to have won the calm of resignation, which
comes to women only as the mournful heritage of dead hope and passion."

I looked at her with some surprise, but
while I hesitated how to reply, Sybil re-
entered the room, and Miss Hogge abruptly
changed her tone.

"Ah, here is our young lady again !
Have you had your laugh out, my dear, at
the old maid ? I am going now, so you
may laugh at your ease."

Then she held out her hands, and taking
both of mine, again fixed her eyes so in-

tently on my face, that for a moment I feared she was going to kiss me. I need not have been afraid, for, as I afterwards heard, Miss Henny had been known to boast that she had never in her life kissed a child or—a woman! She dropped my hands, and turned to Sybil.

"Good bye, little Miss Giggleums. May Wharnecliffe, my dear, come and see me soon, but do not bring her with you. I don't care for slips of girls who have not come to sense yet! Don't pout, child; with such a face as yours, you will have sense enough to please the wisest man for a long time yet, and that is as much as you will ever care to have, maybe."

"Oh, what a horrid woman!" was Sybil's exclamation, before the door had well closed on our eccentric visitor; then, stopping with a kiss the reproof that hovered on my lips,—

"Now, you darling, you are going to scold me! I confess I was very rude, but how could any one help laughing at such an unconscionably ridiculous old figure?"

"*I* did not laugh, Sybil; and I should have hoped that my little sister's sense of the ridiculous would have been less powerful with her than the fear of giving pain."

The sweet face clouded instantly.

"I did not give her pain, May. No, a woman could not make such an exhibition of herself if she minded being laughed at."

"That does not follow, my child, but in future, I wish you to see in any of our visitors not a lay figure to criticise, but a possible friend to welcome."

"I will try, May dear," she answered, and drooped her long lashes penitently ; but the next minute she glanced archly from beneath them. " I will indeed, Mite, but oh ! I do hope there are not many such objects in Kelvydon !"

CHAPTER VII.

A STATE VISIT.

MISS HOGGE took the bad weather away with her, for the next day came brilliant spring sunshine and balmy airs, whereupon our neighbours arrayed themselves and their drawing-rooms in chintzes and muslins, and fluttered forth, gay as butterflies, to welcome us. There was, however, nothing remarkable either in their manners or their toilets to provoke Sybil's merriment; indeed, now that sunlight sparkled on the crimson tassels of the larches, and the golden mosses in the woodland paths, she was out constantly, rambling among the coppices in search of primroses and anemones, and did not see much of my visitors.

What a mere child she was! how entirely she threw herself into the pleasures of her young life, the innocent pleasure of mere being, which she shared with the birds and the flowers! With her foot on the threshold of womanhood, how little does she foresee the absorbing interests, the passionate joys and sorrows, that may lie but a step beyond.

She is even as regardless of her beauty as a bird of the tints of its plumage, yet surely the day will come when this gift, so precious to a woman, will assert its true value to her, when, in right of it, she sees herself a queen?

For a moment, I fancied the revelation had come, when our curate, Mr. Mervyn, called on his return from Dorset. He was a quiet, gentlemanly-looking young man, with silky hair and whiskers, and the large dark eyes, which many girls think so irresistible, and those languishing eyes were so often, and so expressively turned on Sybil; his voice took such a low, soft tone, when he addressed her that really I began to think of the possibilities that *will* suggest themselves when one sees a handsome young man evidently attracted towards a pretty girl.

There happened to be some greenhouse plants in the window, that Lassie had cherished all the winter into early bloom, and had insisted upon bringing from London with her, and Mr. Mervyn asked her, in such a lackadaisical tone to give him "just one blossom, to inaugurate the spring for me." As ill-luck would have it, there were only two flowers in bloom—a small crimson rose and a staring, yellow gazania, and I could scarcely suppress a laugh when Sybil, with perfect gravity, presented him with the gazania, and he went away with it in his coat, where it looked like a great brass button!

But when I watched the little maiden as she stood at the window, her eyes pensively following his retreating figure, for a moment I confess that my heart trembled presage-fully.

Only for a moment,—she turned away from the window.

"It was so selfish of me," she said; "I could not pluck my *only* rose, and I am so sorry; but the milky sap of that gazania will spoil the poor man's coat, and perhaps it is his best. I am so sorry!"

And then, forgetting Mr. Mervyn and his flower, she threw her arm round me, and

drew me away to the brook at the end of
the garden, to watch a shoal of tiny silver
fishes, which, I fancy, were only minnows,
although she insisted that they were baby
trout.

We were so intent, she, in diving her
plump white hand to the elbow in the water,
trying to capture the glittering prey, and I
in holding back her skirts, lest she should
get wet and take cold, that neither of us
heard a footstep stealthily coming down the
walk, until a laughing voice behind us said—

"Good luck to your fishing, ladies ; Miss
Wharnecliffe, are you afraid that the envious water-witch will steal your young sister
from you ?"

Colonel Brereton's glance at Sybil, as he
asked this question, gave it significance,
indeed, any river-sprite might well have been
envious of the bright face that looked

round at him, with flushing cheek and startled eyes.

" Forgive me for interrupting you in such an exciting amusement," he continued, when I had cordially returned his greeting, "and forgive me this freedom of coming to you unannounced. I have brought Mrs. and Miss Stacy to see you. They are waiting in the drawing-room !"

" And, oh, Sybil ! your dress has dipped into the brook, and all your hair is falling down ! do go in through the dining-room and make yourself presentable."

But Sybil, heedless of my visitor, or his announcement, was again absorbed in her piscatory pursuit, and only looked up to say, " Mrs. Stacy does not want me, does she, Colonel Brereton ? I must have one of these little slimy fellows before the shoal swims past." And thereupon she made a dive, which would infallibly have precipitated her into the river had I not caught her, I am shocked to confess it, by the leg!

Colonel Brereton laughed, and turned modestly aside, while I whispered angrily, "Go in instantly, Sybil, change your dress, and come into the drawing-room like a gentle-woman. How can you be such a hoyden!"

"She is wild with the excitements of her new life," I said apologetically to my friend, as I accompanied him back to the house; if she does not steady down soon, I am afraid that Mrs. Grundy of Kelvydon will be scandalised at such a result of a "London boarding-school" education.

"Never mind Mrs. Grundy," replied Colonel Brereton, "Sybil is charming, 'without any control but the sweet one of gracefulness,' which her nature cannot break through."

Very kind of him to say so, but no girl can look graceful with her head in the water and her heels in the air !

Mrs. Stacy was a slight and rather elegant woman, dressed in the height of the fashion and in a style a little too youthful for her age, although her slender figure and delicate features palliated, if they did not justify the error. Her companion, Constance Stacy, was a tall girl of twenty, with fair hair and very prominent eyes, and a general limpness about her figure, which, with many people, might stand for grace.

The elder lady was very affable ; she explained that her husband would have accompanied her, but that he suffered much from asthma, and rarely quitted his house.

" So I have brought your old friend Colonel Brereton, as his representative, or rather he has brought me, Miss Wharnecliffe, as it is through him that I have the pleasure of becoming acquainted with you."

" And having prepared that kind office for you, madame," said the Colonel, " I will leave you to profit by it, while I run over for a chat with my dear crony, Miss Henny Hogge, or I shall get into disgrace with her, and I am not bold enough to risk the consequences."

" Well,—don't be long, John, please ; the admiral will be nervous if we are late home ;" and, after a little hesitation, she added : " You will tell Miss Henny from me, that I shall be in town again soon, and will call on her then."

" All right," answered the Colonel,—and when he had disappeared Mrs. Stacy turned to me.

" So glad that you are to be a neighbour of ours. Plaistow is seven miles from

Woodglen ; but here we do not think much of a seven miles' drive for a pleasant visit. Do you know, I think I met a relation of yours—a brother, perhaps,—in town, last spring ? "

" Of mine ?—Scarcely, I think, since I have no surviving relatives, to my knowledge. I am very poor in that respect, Mrs. Stacy."

" He might have been a distant one ; still, as the name is so uncommon.—Constance, you remember Captain Wharncliffe, whom we met,—no, by the way, it was in Paris we met him,—last spring ? "

Constance looked perplexed.

" You have surely not forgotten him, my love ? You danced with him twice. At the Embassy, you recollect ? He came with the Marchioness of Hylif's party."

" Oh, mamma !—You are mistaken,—

that man's name was Warner, not Wharnecliffe ! "

" Warner, was it ?   How stupid of me !
I certainly thought the dear marchioness
said his name was Wharnecliffe.   I beg
your pardon, Miss Wharnecliffe."

And satisfied with this ingenious method
of impressing upon me the great in-
equality that must naturally exist between a quondam school-mistress and a
lady who met marchionesses at ambas-
sadors', Mrs. Stacy changed the subject to
the usual conversational trivialities of a
·morning call, while Miss Stacy sat silent,
rolling her wan eyes on me from time to
time, with a languid expression of friendly
interest, until Sybil came in, when my
visitor stopped abruptly, and put up her
gold eye-glass to examine her.

" Your sister ?   I was not aware—true,
Colonel Brereton told me you had a sister ;

but I fancied, from what he said, that she
was quite a child."

And she gazed at Lassie with an expression almost of dismay, but soon recovered
herself, and dropping her glass with careless
graciousness, went on—

"You must come to Plaistow soon, both
of you, my daughters will be charmed with
such a companion. You are musical, I
see," — glancing at the piano, which was
strewn with songs which Sybil had been
practising,—"That is delightful! Will not
Maria be delighted, Constance?"

She went to the piano to inspect the
music pieces. Sybil followed, and as they
were turning them over, Miss Stacy
addressed me.

"Have you seen much of Cousin John
since he returned to England, Miss Wharnecliffe?"

"Nothing at all, until we met acci-

dentally, when I was on my way to Woodglen."

The wan eyes brightened a little.

" I thought you were so very intimate.
He has told us how good you were to his
poor little child who died. I believe he
was very young when he married, and his
marriage was rather a mésalliance, so that
cousin Fanny was not much with his family,
and, of course, he felt your kindness to her
all the more."

Not knowing what reply to make to this
rather uncalled-for communication, I remained silent, and the effusive young lady
went on to say—

" Cousin John is like my elder brother—
I have no brothers *all* my own. Mrs. Stacy
is my step-mother—Cousin John's friends
must be mine. You will let me claim you
for one, dear Miss Wharnecliffe?"

Bless me, thought I, what affectionate people these S—shire folk seem to be. I have only been arrived a fortnight, and already I have the offer of two new friendships, and the confirmation of an old one! I made some gracious reply to Miss Stacy's unexpected overtures, and then her mother-in-law came forward, looking restlessly at her watch.

"Constance, your cousin is forgetting time in Miss Henny's society; that is always the way; she has no respect for other people's engagements."

"She is a great friend of Colonel Brereton's, is she not?" I asked.

"Oh, yes!—it is very strange, but she really does contrive to get quite a little clique of gentlemen about her. She amuses them,—which is all that idle men care for. Poor woman, she is much to be pitied, but it is impossible to take much notice of a person whose manners are so *brusque,* and whose dress is so eccentric, though she exacts a great deal of attention on the strength of her father and brother's long residence in the neighbourhood,—where, I believe, they were highly respected."

Our visitor waited a little longer; but the Colonel not making his appearance, she rose.

" Constance, my dear, we must bid the Misses Wharnecliffe good-bye. I will drive round by Miss Hogge's, and send in for the Colonel." (Then lowering her voice a little.) " I never take my girls into Miss Hogge's society, when I can avoid it without offence, and I warn you against trusting your sister much with her. Poor thing, she is decidedly a freethinker. Dr. Hogge was almost an infidel,

and she has imbibed his habits of thought,
I fear."

" I am not afraid for Sybil," I answered,
as I thought of that young lady's unflatter-
ing comment on her new acquaintance ; but
as Mrs. Stacy and her step-daughter sailed
softly to their carriage, I remembered the
wistful pathetic look, underlying all the
flash and sparkle of Miss Henny's eyes,
and I did not believe Mrs. Stacy's asser-
tions, and I remembered there was an old
quarrel.

I sighed, and Sybil drew near, and
taking my face in both her dimpled hands,
said :

" That is the second sigh you have
breathed since morning, little May."

She called me "little," in right of her
two inches superiority of stature, as I called
her "little," in right of my seniority.

" And now I look at you, there is a droop round your mouth, and a mist in your eyes, such as I always notice when, when—you are anxious or unhappy. I do believe you are disappointed, because that splendid Mrs. Stacy has whisked away our *cavalier seul*, — that charming ' Johnnie,' as his friend Miss Hogge calls him."

" I rather think, Sybil, that he whisked himself off, and that Miss Hogge is more to blame than Mrs. Stacy for our loss ; but, assuredly, I was not sighing over *that.*"

" Why do you sigh at all ? Happy people never sigh ; after all, you are not happy in this beautiful Woodglen. Not happy, alone with me! You are pining for the old school-days, and for the noisy girls who used to tease and pet you ? I tell you what ! I'll write for Jenny Colvin

to come at once ! You will be more content
with our pretty home, when there are
more faces you have been used to around
you ? "

" Nonsense, Lassie,—Jane cannot come
till Midsummer, and I was not sighing for
myself—and, Sybil, dear child, you must
not pry too curiously into the source of
every smile and sigh of those who love you
best, lest they learn to hide from you what
you cannot always share."

My sister gazed at me for a moment with
a soft wistfulness in her violet eyes ; but
the cloud passed quickly, and she tripped
gaily to the door.

" It is time nearly for your tea. You are
always low-spirited when you want your tea.
I shall go and see after that snail Bessie, and
make her send it."

As she left me, I sighed again,—and this

time the sigh was for myself. The child has guessed rightly. I am not so happy as I ought to be, — I feel lonely and dissatisfied. Surely, I miss my pupils, my old hard work. If there was a spiritual post-office in the world, to forward all the letters *mentally* written, before or after those outwardly dispatched, what different results would follow! When I wrote to Thorold, a few days after his last letter reached me, I felt and expressed, only a loving thankfulness for his tender words, and a joyful anticipation of the re-union that shall crown his long fidelity.

But since then I have read and re-read his letter with ever-increasing dissatisfaction. Now that he is free to rejoin me at once—at any moment—why should he linger to arrange his business matters? Why should a profit in the sale of some

sheep be of more importance to him than
the earliest possible meeting with her who
has lived only on the hope of it for eleven
weary years? What could have kept me
from him if the restraint had been one
that I could at choice have broken through?
"Only one year longer," he writes, and
life is so short. Another year to pine and
watch through—a dull, gray year, which
might have been one long summer of glad
fruition.

Ah, Thorold, would it seem a little
thing to the prisoner whose longing eyes
are turned to his momentarily opened grat-
ing, that it should be reclosed and barred
against him, and all the blessed light extin-
guished from him—though "only for one
year more?" You cannot have suffered as
I have done, my love, or for all the flocks
and herds that ever browsed, you would

not prolong this " long, long anguish of patience when a word of yours could end it."

I begin to think Thorold may be right after all in the taunts with which he used playfully to vex me, at feminine weakness and narrowness. Small thanks he owes me for trusting him when I could do nothing else, if at the first check I turn upon him with accusation and reproach.

There, it is over now. I am once again what you have often called me, Thor— ' your own patient little May.' But I foresee that for many reasons, this last year of probation will be hard to bear. First, I am idle, and shall miss the great solace of work. I shall have too much leisure for dreaming. Then, I cannot settle to my changed life and my new home when I feel that

they are mine for "only one year longer."
And I seem further from Thorold here than
I did in Bedford Square. That dingy parlour was made sacred to me by our last
parting. Standing on the spot where I
received his last embrace—where his last .
look dwelt on me—I could feel sometimes that his spirit was reaching forth
to find me, and that mine responded to
his call "Yes, Thorold, I am here."
But—

"Oh, Sybil, how can you bounce into a
room in that way? You forget what Miss
Colvin used to tell you that ' self-restraint
is the soul of good breeding !"

"Then," retorted Sybil, saucily, "Colonel
Brereton is a very ill-bred person, for I am
sure he does not practise self-restraint in
calling on a lady twice in the same day.
I saw him from the passage window cross-

ing the street, and—there he is at the door !"

And before I could answer, there he was, in the room.

CHAPTER VIII.

THE COLONEL COMES BACK.

"MISS WHARNECLIFFE, I take the privilege of old acquaintance, to ask you for a cup of tea. You dine early, I know; I reckoned on finding you at this hour at the tea-table."

"But how is it you have not gone back to Plaistow with Mrs. Stacy?"

"I had one or two commissions to do for the Admiral, and Miss Henny's seductive society made me forget them, until Madam called for me in a prodigious hurry, so I told her I would stay in

10—2

Kelvydon and walk back to Plaistow. It
is only five miles over the hills—if I don't
start till eight, I shall be there within
regulation hours."

"But have you done all you had to do
in the town? for I will not encourage idle-
ness. You must have been very quick
about it."

"Well, if I must confess the truth,
there was very little to do. I am afraid
my excuse to Mrs. Stacy was not quite in-
genuous. I had resolved to spend this
evening with you, if you do not forbid it.
You hesitate. You fear the Kelvydon
Mrs. Grundy? But, as the children say,
it is only for this once. I promise it
shall not be an established precedent."

"Well, on that condition.'

Indeed, I was glad of the interruption his
arrival made in my too melancholy musings

—and we were soon as merry and sociable as if we had sat at one table every week for years.

" It is like old times come back to see you at my tea-table, as you used to be nine years ago."

It was an awkward observation of mine, and I regretted it as soon as it was spoken.

" Old times," he said, "never come back ; life's law of mutability is too incessant in its action to leave any renewal of them possible—even to imagination."

"The law of mutability," I answered, " is the law not of life, but of death in life—the only real infinite life is that which changes not—and faith and love are its pulsations."

"You are as staunch a Conservative as ever," he smiled ; " will you like the idea of change better if we call it progress—development ?"

"No, indeed; so thoroughly do I hate every form of change, that I would keep my rose always in the bud; my moon, always in the crescent."

"Some do; but they are those whose treasure is 'turned from a toy to a relic, and seen through the crystal of tears.'"

I knew he was thinking of *his* lost treasure—the little golden head that had fallen asleep on my bosom—and there was a silence.

I lifted my eyes to the mirror opposite to admire my sister, as she stood leaning on the back of my chair, in her customary attitude—her hands clasped round my neck, and her polished chin resting on the top of my head, while her deep blue eyes dwelt on our guest in pitying silence.

Her richness of bloom and contour made me look quite wan and wasted, and there

was never much to spare of me at any time.
But I am Thorold's May flower still! Before his return the sweet woodland breezes
will have freshened these faint roses in my
cheeks; and rest and freedom from the
"carking cares" of empty money-bags will
call back the dimples which he used to say
were made to hide kisses in. I smiled as
I remembered that foolish fond saying of
his, and Colonel Brereton caught the smile,
and, of course, misinterpreted it. I was
sure he did from his look, and I broke
silence to say, "By the way, Colonel Brereton, the friendship between Miss Hogge
and you seems to be of great antiquity, to
judge by the familiarity with which she
speaks of you."

"It is very old; it dates from the time
when I was a sickly little lad at Chailey
Grammar School, where her brother, long

since dead, was head master, and it has
outlived many friendships that promised
a longer vitality. Do you know, Miss
Wharnecliffe, you have made quite a conquest of Miss Henny, and you should be
proud of it, for she rarely expresses un-
qualified approval of one of her own sex."

" I do not know what she could have
seen in me, to distinguish me more worthily."

" It was probably that she saw in your
reception of her no signs of repulsion or
ridicule of the undeniable singularity of
her appearance."

" Nay, that is a simple effect of the com-
monest courtesy ; she cannot, in the most
limited intercourse with gentlewomen, be
unused to that."

Here there was a slight pressure on the
top of my head, from the chin of the con-
science-stricken penitent behind me.

" You little guess the extent of Henny's
penetration," answered the Colonel, " if you
think it would have failed to detect your
real feeling, under any assumed courtesy.
I wonder at your tolerance, myself, for
ladies, in general, view any eccentricity in
their own sex with as much hostility as the
wild fowl displays towards ' the speckled
bird,' to which the prophet likened himself."

" I believe that is because they usually
believe that it is an affectation assumed to
attract attention, which, as we are a jealous
race, we always resent. I have never
shared that view. Any, the slightest, de-
parture from conventional standards, is so
entirely against a woman's interest, that
her endeavour will always be rather to conceal eccentricity than to display it ; and I
have never known a *happy* woman who has
not found the effort in some degree practi-

cable. I feel, therefore, only a deep pity when a defiant attitude before the world betrays warfare and struggle in the inner life. The trees of the primeval forest grow straight towards the sky; only on the barren moor, or on the bleak hill-side, we find them gnarled and twisted."

Here Sybil broke in.

"You knew Miss Hogge (what a hateful name) years ago, Colonel Brereton; what was she like then?"

"Like nothing on earth, but herself, even then," he replied; "her toilette, it is true, was twenty-five years younger as to fashion; but I am told, Sybil, that with ladies it makes little difference whether a fashion is twenty-five years, or twenty-five days, out of date. She used frequently to visit Chailey, and we boys all loved her, as 'a right down good fellow,' for her joy-

ous sympathy with all our pursuits and
interests. She might have been a boy herself, so cordially did she enter into them.
Even when Mr. Hogge died, and was succeeded by a stranger, she still kept up her
friendly relations with the scholars; and I
am not the only one of them who has retained his regard for her until this day.
But when her father's blindness kept her
in close attendance on him, and the loss of
her lover . . . . "

"Her lover ! !" repeated Sybil, in amazement.

Colonel Brereton looked at her, and
laughed.

"Do you marvel that Miss Henny ever
had such a possession, little maid? What
will you say when you hear not only that
she loved a man some years younger than
herself, a weakness (turning to me) of which

ladies are more intolerant than we men—
but that he returned her affection passion-
ately; and though he afterwards married
a young and pretty girl, he declared to a
friend, almost on his death-bed, that no
woman had ever supplanted her for a moment in his affections, or weakened the fasci-
nation she had exercised over him."

"Then why did he marry any one else?"
was Sybil's matter-of-fact rejoinder.

"That is a 'why' that is often asked,
Sybil. The engagement had been a long
one, and was likely to be longer, as Henny
could not forsake her old blind father; and
in weariness, perhaps hopelessness, he allowed himself to be persuaded by his own
parents to woo and win the daughter of a
wealthy mill-owner, who was supposed to
be able to line her wedding-dress with bank
notes."

" I hope he was disappointed !" I cried, viciously.

" After a time he was. The father-in-law became bankrupt, the lady's fortune vanished, and much of her husband's with it. He returned with her and his children to Kelvydon, broken in health, ruined in prospects—and Henny was revenged."

" But what brought him to Kelvydon ?"

" That I cannot say. Perhaps the yearning of a dying man, for the scenes of lost youth and happiness. Perhaps the magnetic attraction of the influence his first love had exercised over him, or, possibly, only the wish for retirement and economy."

" And how did Henny take her revenge ?"

" Most nobly. Her father was then dead, leaving her with a rather straitened income. Her former lover was dying of a lingering disease in poverty and privation, aggravated by the ignorant profusion of his wife, who, brought up in extravagant luxury, was unable to meet the necessities of her altered position. No sister could do more for a loved brother, than Henny did for the man who had deserted her in his prosperity. She denied herself comforts to procure luxuries for him, she cheered the repining wife, she amused the fretful children, she soothed his dying bed, and received, as a sacred bequest, the charge of his widow and orphans."

"Ah! that was true fidelity! and the widow?"

"Well, Henny had not the care of her long. She rallied, married a rich man six months after her husband's death, and Henny never forgave it her; indeed, Henny herself was never quite the same afterwards. She grew more brusque in her manner, more careless in her attire, more bitter and cynical in her humour; she took to snuff-taking too,——"

"Oh! Colonel Brereton!" interrupted Lassie, "you should not have told us that. Snuff-taking spoils all the romance!"

" I do not wonder," I remarked, pensively, " that Henny resented the widow's re-marriage—if she could forgive him, she would be the more indignant at her rival's inconstancy; do they ever meet now?"

Colonel Brereton laughed.

" They met to-day, and *you* met the lady also."

" I? Is it Mrs. Stacy? Oh, then I can understand. Come, Lassie, enough of gossip or romance for to-night; let Colonel Brereton hear you sing. She can sing like a very nightingale, Colonel."

Sybil went to the piano in the inner room, opening with folding doors from the

one in which we sat, and presently the air
was filled with the melody of her young
pure voice.

Colonel Brereton stood beside her until
she ceased to sing, and began playing
some lively music; then he returned
to me where I sat, quietly occupied in
cutting out a lamp-shade. He watched
me for a while in silence, and then said
abruptly,—

" How I envy you that sweet child, Miss
Wharnecliffe. If my Fanny had lived, she
would have been just such a blooming
maiden now."

" I wish," I said thoughtlessly, " that I
could share my treasure with you, my dear
friend."

" You can, if you will—do."

I looked up, startled, met his eyes, and
looked down again, feeling myself turn

scarlet as a peony, and cutting a huge hole in my lamp-shade.

Emboldened by my silence, he drew nearer, and bent over me, saying, in a low tone,—

"When you pronounced my sentence, in Bedford Square, I submitted without appeal, because there was something in your manner that gave me the impression that it was irreversible, as it could only be from *another* having been more fortunate than I. But finding you still free, after the lapse of so many years, hope revives again. Maimed and disfigured as I am, I should not have ventured to say this, but for the faint, very faint encouragement of what you said on the platform, which I have cherished——"

Here the music came to a sudden stop, and a dead silence followed. Sybil twirled round on her music stool and faced us.

Doubtless we looked—as I, for one, felt—uncommonly foolish; for, with the ready tact that is instinctive in young girls in such a situation, she wheeled round again to the piano, and dashed off into a noisy "fantasia" under cover of which I regained my self-possession, and answered my suitor. "Your first impression was a true one, Colonel Brereton, I was not then—I am not now—free to give you more than the friendship which I hope will always have some value to you."

"Is it so ?" he said, and I must admit that he looked more interested than mortified. "Forgive me, if I have seemed to force a reluctant confidence."

"Before many months have passed, it will have ceased to be a confidence, and meanwhile I know it will be inviolate with you."

"And you will not think that by my

presumption I have forfeited all the arrears
of an old friendship, that have been due to
me, since we last parted ?" He held out
his hand. I looked up in his face. His
smile was so frank and genial, that all my
embarrassment fled for evermore, and I
gave him my hand with a smile, as frank as
his own.

Sybil looked round again, and rose from
the piano, "Are you going away?" said
she, not very hospitably.

"Yes; good bye, I shall see you both
soon again, for Plaistow Manor is my home
for the present, though I leave it to-morrow
for a week or two. When I come back,
Sybil, I shall find you and my pet cousin,
Conny Stacy, close friends, I hope."

When he was gone, my naughty little
sister observed, "Miette, I hope you do not
mean to set yourself up as *my* duenna;

11—2

whereas it is very clear, that it is I who am to be yours. And a hard duty I am likely to find it. I must send for Jenny Colvin to help me, if this is the way you are going on."

I made some careless reply, and the child did not pursue the subject, reserving it, doubtless, for her letters to Laura Tresham.

But certainly I did think it very hard that a lady of my years could not have a quiet conversation with a middle-aged gentleman in her own parlour, but that because he was once her lover, he should fire off a second proposal at her in that way! Not a very fiery proposal, certainly—just a thin ghost of that ardent avowal of nine years ago. But time and absence work changes —except in the one loyal and changeless, my own Thorold.

CHAPTER IX.

MISS HENNY " CHEZ ELLE."

" SYBIL dear," I said to her, a few days after the Colonel's visit, " I am going to see Miss Hogge, but you know, she told me I was not to bring you, so you must amuse yourself in the garden until I come back."

" Oh, May, I must have a walk this lovely morning! May I go across to Dr. Barnes? Miss Boyden (Mrs. Barnes' governess) is going to take the children to Lyndon Park, and I want to go with her. She says there are such lots of primroses and

'wooden Emilys' as little Lucy calls them
there."

"Lyndon Park! where is that? who
lives there?"

"It is over the hill, towards Plaistow.
No one lives there, except the gardener,
and a housekeeper. May I go?"

"Yes, if you like, but, Sybil, do not be
wild and stay out late, to get Miss Boyden
scolded. Be sure to be home before tea
time."

. Sybil promised duly, and I left her at
the doctor's door, and went on to Miss
Hogge's. Her house was in a narrow back
street of the town, leading down to the
river, and in a row of cottages inhabited by
the better class of artisans and mechanics.
It had nothing to distinguish it from its
neighbours, except a very bright brass
knocker and bell handle, and ground glass

in the lower windows, by way of substitute
for the spotted or checked muslin blinds,
more or less clean and pretentious, that
marked the "parlours" of the adjoining
tenements. This exterior not being very
prepossessing, it was an agreeable surprise
to find the door opened by a neat little
maid-servant, who showed me at once into
the room with the ground-glass windows,
with what had been folding-doors, now
papered over, at one end ; and murmuring
something about "telling Missus," she
retired. Not very far, however, for the
next minute I heard her speaking in a sub-
dued tone, on the other side of the parti-
tion, and then Miss Hogge's voice, raised
to a higher than its usual key, enquired,

"What do you say ? why do you mutter
like that, child ? who is it ?"

The girl's reply was still inaudible.

" Miss Wharnecliffe ? well, you need not
mumble her name so ; I daresay she is not
ashamed of it, or she would have got rid of it
before now.   Put your cap straight, it is all
on one side.   Young girls ought never to
be slatternly."

Perhaps Miss Henny thought that was
a privilege reserved for *old* girls, and if so,
she availed herself of it to the uttermost.
She looked as if her toilet had been
arranged on the principle of plunging her
into an old clothes bag, and bringing her
up, with such of its contents as would stick
to her.   Indeed, as to shape, colour, and
texture, her dress might have been the bag
itself.

On her head was a lace cap, which might
once have been costly, but looked as if it
never *could* have been clean, and under it
she wore some shaggy braids of false hair,

from beneath which her own grey locks curled and twisted so that to a classical fancy, she might have looked like Medusa with a wig on. And still strangely out of keeping with these coarse "personnels" were small white hands, delicate, and well cared for, and still the plaintive look, underlying the restless brilliance of the large black eyes.

"This is kind of you, to come to me so soon," she began, "but where is your sister?"

"You told me not to bring her, Miss Hogge."

"Did I?" (and her eyes twinkled slyly); "that was rude of me, but it is no pleasure to merry girls to visit old maids, and they are a restraint on conversation, besides. What does she do when you leave her?"

"She is gone to Lyndon Park for primroses, with Miss Boyden, and the little Barneses."

"Ah, the sweet innocents! may they long find pleasure in gathering primroses— by themselves! But it is a good hour's walk from Lyndon, they can't be back for an hour. Will you stop with me, and we will have a good feast of gossip?"

I hesitated. The gossip might, or might not, have been a temptation; but the cottage was so lonely, when Lassie was not in it. My neighbour took my hesitation for consent.

"There that's right, you are a good little creature, we shall be great cronies, I see. We won't sit here though, this is my reception room, you shall be made free of my inner sanctuary, I only receive company here; the naughty little boys look into the room—there! you see?"

And in fact, at that instant, a grimy little countenance was discernible, peering over the permanent blinds; but at a menacing gesture from my hostess, it abruptly disappeared.

"After all," she continued, "I don't much object to boys *outside* the window. It is our duty to contribute to the people's innocent amusements, and what can be more innocent for a boy, than staring into a room with nobody in it ? So cheap too !"

As she ran on thus, she led the way across a narrow passage to the door of the room communicating with the one we had quitted. She went in first, and I followed her, but recoiled on the threshold in surprise and dismay, for the most prominent object in the little dark, stuffy apartment, was a great oak coffin, placed on the floor, under the window, and taking up the whole side of the wall. I glanced enquiringly at my companion, and met her black eyes fixed piercingly on mine, with a gleam of mischievous merriment in them.

"What is the matter, my dear ? Oh,
the coffin, is it ? You are not superstitious,
I hope ? it has stood there these twenty
years."

Mastering my momentary repugnance, I
walked quietly into the room, without
further remark, and took the chair my new
friend offered me ; then I looked round.

It was a dark small parlour, with a window looking on a narrow walled court,
garnished with floating banners of linen hung
out to dry. There seemed to have been a
grand laundry performance in the street.
There were old engravings on the walls, and
old books on the book-shelves. On the
mantel-piece, there was a meerschaum pipe,
and a box of cigars ; a snuff-box was on the
table, and on the floor, beside Miss Hogge,
was a large basketful of newspapers, which
she was shredding into small bits, into

another basket at her feet. She offered me a newspaper, saying, "You will help me with my work, I am sure, and we can chat all the more at our ease."

" Of course, I will help you with pleasure ; but what is this paper mince-meat for ?"

Henny's eyes twinkled mischievously, and her voice took an oily smoothness, as she replied, " I am doing it for a young friend of mine, a district visitor, who takes a deep interest in the poor. These bits of paper are to stuff pillows for them !"

I looked up in surprise, but she went on, " It is so kind of the rich to teach the poor economy—it is a saving on both sides. What can be cheaper than paper pillows ? and they are as comfortable as feathers, if you don't mind the crinkling of them in your ears—or say they are not *quite* so comfortable, still, if a man or woman has been

working as hard all day as he or she ought
to do, why they can sleep on anything !"

" In that case," I ventured to say, " they
might sleep without pillows !"

" Ah, but poor people *will* crave luxuries,
it is the perversity of human—even *poor*
human nature, and it is a great thing to
give them inexpensive luxuries.   Then the
kind feeling it shows in rich people who
sleep on down beds, spending their precious
time in tearing paper pellets for the use of
their *humble* friends.   *Humble,* that is the
word—the present of a paper pillow must
be a great encouragement to humility, if the
acceptance were not a proof of it."

" But," I said, in some perplexity, " if you
do not approve of the work, why do you
undertake it ?"

" I disapprove ?—not at all.   I have
nothing particular to do, and have not the

least objection to oblige dear Maria Gibson.
Cheap labour, and cheap materials, the
result must be satisfactory !"

Then suddenly changing her manner—.
"It is real love for you, May Wharnecliffe, that makes me admit you here—I
seldom allow women to come into this, my
bachelor parlour.   Dr. Barnes comes sometimes of an evening, when he can escape
from his wife's eternal chatter about the
servants and the babies—he smokes that
meerschaum.   Julius Mervyn comes to dis-
course about his parish work, and his love
affairs ; Johnnie Brereton sits with me and
tells me about his little dead daughter, and
we laugh over old stories of Chailey school
days.   Johnnie is always as much interested in his friends' affairs, as in his
own ; but my circle is narrowing fast ; the
old rector is in his dotage nearly, and old

Admiral Stacy is kept at home by his
' stuck up' wife, who persuades him that
his health requires coddling all the winter,
but you are the only woman I suffer here !"

"To what do I owe the privilege ?" I
asked, smiling, "I hope to nothing very
masculine in my appearance ?"

"Masculine ? you little dot, you, with
your silver voice, and soft calm eyes ! How
those eyes keep wandering to that coffin !
It is my poor father's coffin."

I started and dropped my paper. "Of
course," she continued, quite unmoved,
though the malice in her glance betrayed
her enjoyment of my surprise—" of course
he is not inside it ! Poor dear, he is where
he ought to be, in Kelvydon churchyard,
with all his patients round him."

It is to be hoped that his patients did
not all precede him.

" No, he had that coffin made for himself, years and years ago, to familiarise himself with the idea of death, and he used to keep his books and papers in it. But when he died, he had grown far too stout for it, and I keep it partly in memory of him, and also because it is very useful. The servants are so ' skeared ' at it that mine won't go into the room alone after dark, so I keep my bottled beer in it, and the bottles don't burst so often when her cousin comes to visit her."

I did not relish the association of this ghastly " memento mori " with the homely convivialities of bottled beer, so, to change the subject, I enquired if she had admitted Mrs. Stacy into her sanctum, when she called the other day for her friend.

" Mrs. Stacy, indeed! not I! In fact, she never got out of her carriage, but sent

in a message for Johnnie, and he went out
to speak to her. Times are changed, my
dear! When Mrs. Stacy was a widow,
she could not live without me. The old
Admiral (an old imbecile he was and is)
used often to be here, and she would drop
in and consult him about her boys, and admire his little girl. And then before her
husband had been dead a year, or his wife
two, off she sets to London in her crape and
weeds, to come back with the Admiral in
bridal finery, privately married, by special
license, if you please."

I was fain to laugh at the idea of the astute
old maid having been outwitted by the wily
widow ; but Miss Henny resumed the story
of her wrongs.

"And the first thing Madame tried
to do when she was settled at Plaistow,
was to oust me from the society of my
father's old friends. Very gradually, but

I found her out, and from that time it has been war between us; very civil war, but that, you know, is the bitterest."

"Does your enmity extend to Mrs. Stacy's daughters? or do you like them better?"

"Her daughter, Maria Gibson, is a tiresome pedant. Constance, her step-daughter, is a sentimental goose."

"She is rather pretty, don't you think?"

"No, I don't. Are you jealous of her?"

The enquiry was so totally unexpected, that I felt myself colour to the roots of my hair, and my tormentor chuckled.

"That is a very pretty blush, my dear, but there is too much of it for the occasion. Tell me, why did you refuse my dear Johnnie?"

"Who told you that I *had* refused your Johnnie, as you call him?"

" He told me himself nine years ago. Now you see how it is, May Wharnecliffe, that you are no stranger to me. Why, John Brereton has come here—to this very room—and talked of you by the hour."

" I am sorry he could find no worthier topic of conversation."

" He thought then that your refusal of him was dictated by some previous attachment. Yet you are still unmarried, and still refuse him ? He told me that the other night. Men always confide in me."

" Colonel Brereton," I said, laughing, " is more indiscreet about his failures than other men are about their successes, a proof that he does not feel them very deeply."

" That is so like a woman ! You are angry with my poor Johnnie because he is not broken-hearted by your coldness, as, indeed he was, nine years ago."

"But he 'wears his rue with a difference' now, you see, and I certainly am not angry with him for it, although the renewal of his offer was, by his own confession, a kind of after-thought, and no proof of unchanging fidelity."

"Unchanging fiddle-strings. What *is* fidelity if it is not a man's loving one woman for eight or nine years—even in spite of absence?"

"During which period he managed to exist very comfortably, without knowing what had become of me; and meeting me quite accidentally, he took up his passion just where he had dropped it, and being again 'declined with thanks,' he calmly substitutes for it the brotherly regard which, indeed, is for *such* fidelity a very good exchange."

"*Such* fidelity? You know very little

of men, my woman, if you fancy that they
are capable of any long fidelity that will
cost them pain! A man won't rage and
roar about one girl for eight years, if he
has anything else to amuse him. If he
keeps any thought of her in his heart for
so long, you may be sure it is packed away
comfortably in some corner, well padded
with other interests that may not smother
it, but will keep it from flaming up incon-
veniently. Do you really believe that any
man will be separated from a woman for
eight years—eight !—for five ?—for three ?
—and love her when he meets her again
in the same way—to the same degree—as
when they parted ?"

"Of course, I believe it." I answered,
indignantly.

She took a long pinch of snuff, fixing

her eyes keenly on mine the while. "Did you ever hear of such a case?"

"I know,"—I began, and stopped, for there was a triumphant glitter in her eyes that warned me of the trap.

"Well, go on—you know—."

"That it is time for me to say good evening, Miss Hogge."

"Don't call me Miss Hogge; call me Miss Henny, or plain Henny if you like—plain enough I am, I know. Not that I am ashamed of my name. I claim to be royally descended, from 'Og, the King of Bashan.' Mrs. Stacy boasts that her husband's family came in with the Conquest (they didn't bring her with them if they did). I tell her *my* family went out with the Conquest, and a far earlier Conquest too. By the way, do you know any lords?"

"Any —— ?"

"Lords or ladies—any titled people I mean? If you do, you have only to signify that fact to Mrs. Stacy, and she will fall down and worship you, and ask you to dinner or to lunch, according to the degree of your intimacy with the said grandees."

"I am afraid," I answered, laughing, "that I can advance no such claim to her consideration. I know nobody of higher rank than a baronet, and I do not know much of him."

"A baronet may do; he may be worth an early tea perhaps. Who is he? Do you know him well?"

"Oh, no; I have not seen him since he came to his title; he is my—he is Mr.— he is the brother of Sybil's guardian."

My embarrassment was not lost on my

questioner. "Who is Sybil's guardian, and where is he ?"

" He is in New Zealand at present; but really, Miss Henny, I must go now," and I escaped further inquisition for *that* time.

CHAPTER X.

AN ARTIST—I SUPPOSE.

MIDSUMMER close at hand. One quarter already past of the year, which seemed so interminably long in prospect when I first went to Kelvydon, and after all it has slipped quite rapidly away. Colonel Brereton, who often drives over with Constance Stacy to see Sybil, laughs at me, and tells me that after all my professed aversion to change, I take very kindly to it when it is once effected, and that the fascinations of Kelvydon have overcome my longings after Bedford Square.

Certainly, it is pleasant to look round my pretty home and feel that I am free to go about when and where I please, and no longer forced to mete out all my employments by the rule of school discipline and method. I do not even regret my girls, since I keep with me the gem of the circlet—the queen flower of the wreath—in my darling Sybil. My life seems now to have been put back to the happy time, before sorrow and separation had saddened it, and the toil and struggle of the years that followed it, are fading from my memory like the more recent characters on a palimpsest, leaving the old writing legible once more.

The revived associations of my country life are, I think, partly the cause of this.

As I stood this morning training the honeysuckle round the verandah, it seemed not so long ago since I stood on just such a bright June day, tying up the jessamine in my dear father's vicarage garden, while Sybil, a lovely little angel of three years old, implored me to lift her up to peep into a robin's nest I had once shown her there.

All the time I lived in town I had gathered no wild-flowers : the other day I saw some white woodruff in a lane, and back flew my thoughts to the last time I had seen any. I was walking in a coppice, with Thorold, and he *would* twist the scented blossoms in my hair. It was a wreath fit for a fairy bride, he said, and nothing less delicate should deck his little May-queen.

The woodruff is going off now ; when it comes into bloom again, who knows ? my lover may pluck it again for me, though I am too staid now for such girlish freaks as twining flowers in my hair.

How that thrush sings! "Billy Pitt! Billy Pitt!" I was quite cross with Thor for declaring that was what the mavis says, such a ridiculous call for a singing bird! though he protested it was quite as poetical a one as "jug! jug!" for a nightingale. And really he has always seemed to repeat it ever since. Ever since? why for ten years I have not heard a thrush singing on a tree. Surely that must be the same bird that cried "Billy Pitt" to Thorold and me that day. He will cry it to both of us, next year, I hope. But by the time he has done with his next year's nest, Thorold and his little mate will have flown further a-field to build theirs—not I fancy in Kelvydon.

I take out the letter I had from him last night, and read it again all through. It is

not a very long one.   His letters get shorter
and shorter every mail.   If he is to be
away much longer, I think our communica-
tions will be cut down to a telegram, or
to the meagre message which was my
annual allowance during old Sir Edward's
life.

However, I am not complaining.   Active,
practical men, like Mr. Challoner, are seldom
garrulous penmen, and though he notices
what I write to him very briefly, he lets
nothing pass unnoticed ; his letters, if brief,
are generally to the point.

So here I sit alone, beneath the fragrant
woodbine, reading my love's sweet words
to the music of the thrush in the syringa.
Sing, little speckled breast, to your brooding
mate, whose large bright eyes watch you from
under the leaves that tremble to the vibra-
tions of your song.   Boast your fidelity of

a summer, all past and forgotten when the holly-berries redden the winter snows— over a life's fleeted spring time, across a wide world of waters,—my own tried and true love sings to me !

 " MY LITTLE MAY-QUEEN,

  " This letter will find you in your kingdom, reigning, as May-queens should reign, among your birds and flowers. I like better to fancy you among such surroundings, than in that hideous parlour in ' the Square,' with those dreadfully professional ornaments of gaily bound books, and pictures, whose frames judiciously solicited more attention than themselves. And then that wretched little frost-bitten Miss Colvin, with her blue finger-tips and blue nose."

That is Thorold all over—so sensitive to

any lack of feminine charm in the women about him !

"Your improved fortune has evidently made you quite a worldly little woman ; you have grown practical and matter-of-fact from the sweet dreamer you used to be !   I gather that, from the passage in your letter in which you congratulate yourself, and me, that when our marriage is announced to my family, there will be nothing to alarm Sir Franklin's prudence—hang his prudence !—or Lady Harriet's pride, in the position of the lady who will assume their name.   Quite right, my Miette.   Of course, if I must have stooped for my jewel in a cinder-heap, she would have been my jewel still ; but such folk as my brother and his lofty wife like to have their gems in a fashionable setting, from a modish jeweller's shop, and it is as well to conciliate such silly scruples when we can, and laugh at them when we can't.

"But when you carry your felicitations into the subject of Sybil's grace and beauty, I can't say I follow you. What the deuce does it matter that a man's sister-in-law is handsome or plain, provided she looks like a gentlewoman, and 'behaves herself as sich?' It is a tradition of yours that I care so very much for beauty, that I couldn't even eat my dinner, if it had been prepared by an ugly cook" (I never said such a thing, Thor.) "while, with true feminine inconsistency, you aver your confidence that my truth and love for you can be shaken by no change.

"Quite right again, my child, in that last. No change that can pass over you will make you otherwise than lovely in my eyes. Time can never rob my May-flower of her grace and delicacy — her sweet womanly gentleness and modesty, the aroma of the blossom that can survive its bloom. As for Sybil, if she were the prodigy you think her, *I* shall not see much of it, I have too long arrears to pay up, in gazing elsewhere. Perhaps, too, she will have fled from Woodglen, before I get there. While you are 'mooning' and musing, some fellow —the Curate, perhaps, or the one-armed Colonel—will pounce on her and carry her off, before her guardian can hurry to the rescue, with his cry of 'stop thief.' And now for a little business talk, so far as you may be supposed to be able to understand business matters. My brother——"

Here a handful of daisies fell upon the paper. I looked up. Sybil stood in the flowery door-way, and clapped her hands merrily.

" I've caught you, you grim little hermit, you! Hiding yourself here, with your tiresome Zealand letter. I shall be glad when that old creature comes back, to talk what he has to say, instead of making you spoil your pretty eyes by poring over his tedious scrawls. Put it away, Mite, and listen to the news I have brought you."

" What news, Lassie ?"

" Great news—glorious news—that will throw all Kelvydon, nay, all S—shire into excitement—Lyndon Park is sold."

" Who told you ?"

" The gardener's wife at the Lodge told me, and, besides, I saw the new owner thereof, who has come down with some friends to give orders about it."

" You have been there again to-day ; well, when the new owner takes possession, there will be an end to your hunting in his coppices for blue-bells and birds'-nests, and bringing home all kinds of litter to drive the servants frantic."

"Well then, perhaps you are mistaken, Miss Wharnecliffe. I have a special invitation from the new proprietor himself to go there as often as I like, and take what liberties I like with the wild flowers and the wild beasts therein, and I mean to do it."

"So you have seen the new proprietor? I hope you were walking quietly like a lady when he met you, and not scrambling about like a tom-boy, or he would have taken you for one of the 'wild beasts' themselves?"

"It would be an opossum, then, for I was climbing a tree."

"Oh, in that case, as you could advance no pretensions at all to be a gentlewoman, it does not much signify what else he took you for!"

" Ah, the bitter little tongue ! How can you find it in your heart to say such things to your own Me !" And Sybil stroked my hair, and fondled my hand, until further remonstrance was forgotten in a kiss.

" And it was scarcely a tree—only a hawthorn bush. There was a wood-pigeon's nest in it, with two darling ' queechies' in it. Miss Boyden saw them coming, and fled ignominiously, and then they looked up, as they passed, and saw me."

" They—who were they ?"

" Lord Radford and his friend. Don't look so disgusted, Mite. I assure you it was a mere bush, and his lordship assisted me down, so courteously; and I was perfectly self-possessed, and made him an elegant curtsey, a hamadryad could have done no more."

" Probably not so much. I never heard

of . hamadryads being seen climbing—oh,
you naughty girl !"

But as I looked at her, I thought, if Lord
Radford cared for beauty, he would wish to
find such a dryad in every tree.

" Your news may be very exciting for
Kelvydon, Lassie, but it has not much
interest for us. There. can be no social link
between such a swannery as Lyndon Park,
and our wren's nest at Woodglen."

" Oh, but Lord Radford seems very
neighbourly. He asked a great many
questions about the people here, and how
we amused ourselves, and whether I liked
archery and all that."

" As if he cared, you little goose ! I
daresay you looked as shy as could be, and
he good-naturedly tried to put you at your
ease ; by the way, how old is he ?"

· " Oh, ever so old ! He said he had

grand-daughters about my age, and as for wanting to put me at my ease—well, he need not have walked nearly the whole way to Kelvydon with me for that."

"Good gracious !—what next, I wonder ? Lord Radford walked three miles with a chit like you, to talk about archery ? "

"No, not Lord Radford, — did I say Lord Radford ? I meant his friend. His lordship left us, and went off with his man of business, — who met him near the Lodge."

"And Miss Boyden ?—and her pupils ? "

"We lost them somehow; she had run off, as I told you, when she saw the gentlemen coming, and hid herself with the children, who were making cowslip balls in the coppice,—and when I wanted to join her, Lord Radford's friend said she had gone towards the west gate, and he would take

me a short cut through the gardens to meet
her there ; but when we got there, the gate
was locked, and we had to turn back after
all,—and, Miss Boyden having vanished, he
politely escorted me over Furley Hill, as
far as the brook side,—and then, he too
vanished into space,—and so ends my
romance, at which you look as solemn as if
it were a tragedy."

"All very well for once, my pet, but I
shall not let you go roaming with Miss
Boyden any more, if this is the care she
takes of you ! You are too old to scramble
about in this hoydenish fashion, or to
wander about the hills with strange gentlemen."

"One would think, to hear you, May,
that 'strange gentlemen' were swarming
about the hills like caterpillars !—whereas,
this was merely a solitary specimen, come

there quite by accident,—indeed, he told me so himself. There are some rare paintings at Lyndon Park, and Lord Radford brought him down to give his opinion of them, or something of the sort."

" Then he is an artist, I suppose ? Was he old, too ? "

" Not so old as Mr. Mervyn ; but much handsomer, and he had a great deal more to say for himself."

" Hem !—enough of him. Tell me, Sybil, you had a letter from Laura Tresham this morning,—what did she say about coming to us ? "

" Oh, dear !—she says she is afraid she can't come this year, on account of Mary's wedding, which is fixed for Michaelmas,— she cannot leave Mary before then, and she cannot leave Mrs. Tresham immediately afterwards ; but I am to be one of the

bridesmaids. Mary is going to write herself to ask me,—and you will let me go,
Miette, won't you ? "

" Perhaps I may, if you learn to behave
yourself better ; it may be as well for you
to practise as ·her bridesmaid, before you
are called on to officiate—"

I stopped.

" As bride, you were going to say "—
laughed Sybil.

But I was not ; — the words I had
checked on my lips would have completed
the sentence—" Before you officiate as
mine ! "

CHAPTER XI.

ON THINGS IN GENERAL.

THE next morning I left my sister practising a new song that she had borrowed from Maria Gibson, and marched off to have a chat with Miss Henny. My visits to that eccentric personage had become so frequent, that she was almost entitled to claim me (as indeed she did) as her " crony."

The truth is, that partly by direct questioning,—partly by wily stratagem,—she had won from me the cherished secret of my betrothal, before she had known me a fortnight, and now that the time that divided me from Thorold might be reckoned by months, instead of years, it was such a relief to me to have a friend to whom I could pour out all the joy and hope with which my glad heart was overflowing. Miss Henny was *avide* of such confidences, and quite an adept in obtaining them. And yet, I scarcely think she would have won mine, but I was rather more negligent of my secret, since Sir Edward Challoner's death had freed me at least from the promise to keep it. I knew Miss Hogge to be a safe confidante, for she never interested herself in such matters from the moment they were publicly known and commented on, though until then, she hoarded and prized them, as a jackdaw treasures a silver spoon which is only valuable to him, because he can hide it.

To Sybil I still kept silence. She was such a mere child, that the governess instinct which I had imbibed from my long residence with prudish Jenny Colvin,—I had none naturally, I know,—would have restrained me from conversing much with her on such a subject, even had I not felt wishful that Thorold should have some opportunity of winning her confidence and affection before he preferred a brother's claim to it.

But, though I called Miss Henny my "friend," I was far from feeling an entire sympathy with her,—although I do hope I was not so selfish as to seek her society only because she was such a good listener, nor so absorbed in my own prospects, as to be incapable of lively, and even affectionate interest in a character which, with all its oddities and contradictions, pos-

sessed many noble—and some even womanly traits.

Parsimonious in her personal habits, she
was capable of self-denying and unostenta-
tious generosity. Though the follies and
weaknesses of her acquaintance formed the
favourite topic of her unsparing sarcasm, woe
to the unfortunate who ventured to join her
in these sallies, or even manifest too keen
an enjoyment of them! Henny's caustic
tongue was swift to avenge the very wrongs
she had helped to inflict, not unfrequently,
I am sorry to say, with a lack of refinement, and coarseness both of thought and
expression that almost excuses Mrs. Stacy
for declaring—not very politely, in the face
of my intimacy with her foe—that "No
real lady can take pleasure in Miss Hogge's
society." There is more of sadness than of
pleasure in the interest I feel for the lonely

woman, whose existence is so barren of all
that should cheer the declining age of
womanhood,—watching her struggling in
the unequal conflict with the dread pro-
blems of life, which *happy* women put so
lightly by !—and worsted in that conflict,
as her bitter words betray. Her mask of
sneering misanthropy, that hides not the
beating of a passionate human heart,—even
her scepticism—the wistful earnestness with
which she yearns towards the faith and
hope she does not share.

Poor Miss Henny!—she was such a good
daughter, too ! Colonel Brereton tells me
that when a youth, at Plaistow, coming
from late visits to the Kelvydon Rectory,
he has often seen the light in Dr. Hogge's
study window—(he lived in a larger house
than Miss Henny has occupied since his
death)—long after midnight, where she sat

copying mechanically, tedious papers that
she could not understand, and which, when
his eyesight failed, he employed her incessantly in transcribing and reading to him.
When his intellect and his bodily powers
alike failed him, she would suffer no
stranger's tendance, but with her own
hands ministered to him to the last. "She
was very strong then," Johnnie said ; "but
she over-tasked her strength in lifting such
a heavy man as Dr. Hogge to and from his
bed, and was never strong afterwards,
though she never complained."

Some ill-natured people said that she
was too stingy to pay for a nurse ; but she
put up a memorial window in the church
that must have cost more than the wages
of a staff of nurses.

I asked her one day, why she raised
this memento in a church which she

seldom attended ? Her reply was characteristic.

"Because, as people congregate there, it is the best place to put a ' memorial' in, to be sure. *I* don't want anything to remind *me* of my dear father. I am in no danger of forgetting him. Besides, my dear, I like memorial windows—they must be such a comfort to people—there are a few such— who dislike long sermons, and find most sermons long. All that stained glass is such a relief to the eye, and when they are tired of hearing Mr. Mervyn telling them how good they ought to be,—why, they can glance at my dear father's window, and reflect how good he was."

But though I said nothing, I much doubted if the wandering thoughts of Mr. Mervyn's hearers often took the direction of Dr. Hogge's virtues.

Miss Henny was in a bad humour this
morning, I saw it at once in the way she
grunted at me when I entered her parlour,
without looking up from her employment,
which was patching an old velvet boot with
a piece of an older kid glove. I seated
myself beside her, turning my back on that
ghastly cellarette of hers, to which I could
never reconcile myself; but she was "down"
on me at once.

"Don't sit by me, May Wharnecliffe. I
hate people sitting close to me. Go and sit
on the coffin."

I declined the uneasy bench, and meekly
took a chair opposite to her.

Presently she looked up.

"Well!—What have you got to say?
Why don't you say it?"

"So I will, if you will give me that glove
to unpick."

I knew that offer would mollify her, and so it did.

"Then take it, and unpick it carefully. How radiant you look! Ah!—you have had a letter from your god Thor."

"Yes, I have."

"Hand it over to me, I want to see what he says. You won't? That is the way with women and their love-letters,"—(Miss Henny always spoke of 'women' as if she did not belong to the sex)—"they know that the nonsense men think good enough for them would seem absurd—as it is—to any other reader."

"Thorold never writes nonsense to me."

"Then he has ceased to care for you. One great charm of a woman to her lover is, that he can disburden himself to her of all the crudities and trivialities which other

14—2

men would not stop to listen to—all the
dross of thought or feeling, which must be
got rid of somehow, so he shoots it down
before the woman he loves,—and she counts
it all as fine gold."

"And so it is, Miss Henny, when Love
is the alchemist!"

"You are right there. A woman always
begins by trying to persuade herself and
others that 'She loves her love with a P,
because he is Perfect;' but the Alpha and
Omega of his perfections generally turns
out to be, that he thinks *her* so! You
think it is the man you prize? No!—it is
the love with which he flatters you. *He*
may go through as many changes as the
silkworm. Little you care, so long as you
have the silken cocoon, whether it be the
grub or the moth inside it. Will you retain your attachment to Mr. Challoner, if,

when he comes home, he tells you that you
are grown a horrid old fright ?"

" I don't know," I answered, laughing,
" what I might feel if he were so rude as
to *tell* me that, and I should not soon find
out that he *thought* so."

" Because there is as yet no danger !
Come, now, tell me how you get on
with the Plaistow folk, and have you
been much there lately ?. You never
tell me any news; you care only to chatter
about that sweetheart of yours. Don't be
offended. I don't want to offend you. For
all the softness in your voice, and your fair
calm face, there is a curve on your delicate
lips, that tells me, if you were really
offended, you could be inexorable."

" I cannot verify that remark, for I was
never seriously offended with anyone in my
life, and I hope I never shall be. About

the Plaistow folk ?—*I* do not go there often.
Mrs. Stacy is very kind, but too con-
descending for my taste ; but Sybil goes
there a great deal,—she and Miss Stacy are
great friends."

"Does Mrs. Stacy invite her when she
has gentlemen visiting her ?"

"No. I don't think Sybil ever met any
gentlemen there, except Colonel Brereton
and Mr. Mervyn."

"Just so. Mr. Mervyn has no money,
and no church interest. He is labelled
' dangerous ' for such young ladies as the
Plaistow girls ; but he will do very well for
Sybil. His open admiration for her may
serve to keep others at a distance, who
might be more profitably engaged than in
hovering round her. You know how he
admires her."

"Poor Mr. Mervyn ! How can he help

admiring her? But she only laughs at him; he is too sentimental for her. Sybil is all fun and frolic, and has not a spark of sentimentality in her composition."

"I wonder she has not caught some sparks from Constance Stacy then! That girl makes me sick. You should have seen her last week, when I was lunching at the Manor. Johnnie was going to drive me home, and she pretended to faint away because the pony plunged and pranced a little as he came round to the door. I pretended to be as nervous as she was, and I brought her to, by flinging Maria Gibson's aquarium over her—fishes and all! You should have seen how comical she looked, with all the little lobsters kicking in the net upon her hair!"

"Constance—" I began, and stopped. I had my own suspicions of the cause

of Miss Stacy's agitation ; but Henny
was not exactly the person to whom I
would entrust a young girl's secret. However, she caught me up in a minute.

"I know what you are thinking of,—one
need not have very sharp eyes to see that
Conny is goose enough to fancy herself
dying for 'Cousin John;' but she will
languish in vain. Since you refused him he
has got into his head that no woman would
accept his hand, because it is an *odd one !*
He has known Constance from a baby, and
never suspects this new development of her
natural foolishness. 'Talk of—' &c., —
there is the gallant Colonel coming up the
street."

"Oh, then, I will leave you ! I know
you do not like more than one visitor at a
time."

"If you go, he will turn back and walk

home with you, and so I shall not have even one visitor."

This being highly probable, I remained until Colonel Brereton joined us.

" Ah, Miss Henny," said he, " I came expressly to bring you a choice little morsel of news — quite fresh, and here is Miss Wharnecliffe, who has doubtless forestalled me ? "

" I do not suppose she has, unless your news might be contained in a letter from New Zealand."

" It is of more local interest than that. Lyndon Park is sold at last, and Lord Radford, the new proprietor, is going to have it got in order immediately, for the reception of his family. They are in high excitement at Plaistow at the prospect of having a titled neighbour so near."

"Titles are not contagious, are they? is Lord Radford young?"

"Oh, no," I answered, "Sybil tells me that he has grand-daughters of her age."

"Sybil?" repeated Miss Henny reproachfully, "then you knew this—and never told me?"

I apologised most abjectly for the omission, and made all the reparation in my power by relating Lassie's adventure, saying nothing, however, of the hoydenish act in which the gentlemen surprised her, nor of her indiscretion in allowing a stranger to walk home with her, but Miss Henny let nothing escape her.

"Who was the other man with Lord Radford—his son?"

"Scarcely," replied Colonel Brereton; "Lord Radford has only daughters."

"Oh, no," I said, "he is only an artist,

come down to make some arrangement in the picture gallery—at least," I added, correcting myself, " I gathered that from a remark he made to Sybil."

" Can you tell us anything more about the strangers ?" asked Henny ; " you can't ? then you may go away if you like. I cannot spare Johnnie to you this morning." And so I went.

CHAPTER XII.

WHAT I SAW BY THE RIVER-SIDE.

"AND after all," thought I, as I passed slowly out of the narrow, dingy street, into the beauty of the woodland landscape which lay only a few yards beyond—" after all, I never told her that Jane Colvin is coming to Woodglen on Monday, and she will be so indignant, if she has not had due notice to put on her frilled satin gown to call on her!"

I said "gown" advisedly, for it would have been an abuse of language to call Miss Henny's attire " dress."

I half turned to go back to her, thought of Johnnie, and hesitated. Then, the summer air was so sweet and fresh, after Miss Hogge's stuffy room, that was redolent of snuff and sometimes even stale tobacco ! and a stroll by the river would be pleasanter than a renewed contemplation of that gloomy chest of hers, though I had discovered that its contents were—not bottled beer, but Dr. Hogge's old manuscripts.

So I crossed the brook, which the Kelvydonites always called " the river," and wandered for some time along the path beside it, playing all the time with bright fancies, and pleasant memories, and glad hopes, brought to life again—as mirrors and pictures, covered up and shrouded during their owner's absence, are unveiled, and polished up afresh, at the prospect of his return.

At last, recollecting that I had left Sybil

too long alone, I turned back and retraced
my steps, but instead of returning through
the town I followed the path some way
further, between the brook and the wooded
hill, until I came in sight of a little rustic
bridge, which led across the brook to our
garden gate—and then I paused—riveted
to the spot with astonishment at the vision
which met my eyes. Seated on the bank,
under a weeping birch, that drooped its
slender sprays into the passing current—
was my little sister. At her feet lay a
portfolio, and drawings and sketches were
scattered all around her, while, kneeling on
one knee beside her—of course for the better
inspection of the drawing she held before
his eyes—though leaning towards her, much
closer than the occasion demanded, was a
youth of some two-and-twenty summers, in
whose features, no less than in his figure

and attitude, lurked the indescribable air of refinement that would have stamped him, in any circle, as a gentleman, while his dress—a foreign "blouse" belted round his waist—and the easel and palette near him, indicated his occupation at least, if not his profession. The artist! Lord Radford's artist! but how came he there? and—oh! how came Sybil and her portfolio there, beside him?

In the wood! utterly regardless of the serpent tongues of Kelvydon, that would not fail to hiss forth reproach and contumely, if any chance passer-by from that mighty centre of civilisation should happen to behold her! At such appalling indiscretion I sympathised with the parent in the " Beggar's Opera," and "wondered any man alive could ever rear a daughter!"

Yet the group was so pretty, I could not

help pausing to admire it. Sybil had thrown off her hat, and the tremulous shadow of the leaves wavered lovingly on her bare head, and dropped from her lustrous hair, while the sunbeams that twinkled through them seemed laughingly to nestle in the dimples of her sweet rosy lips and ivory chin. What wonder if, as the long curled lashes veiled the eyes that dwelt disparagingly on the drawing in her hand, those of the youth—he was little more than a boy !—were riveted on her face, with that expression—almost of awe—that some eyes wear when they look on perfect beauty. A painter, an artist,—where in all the galleries of Europe could he have met with anything more exquisite, and with all the grace and fragrance of a living bloom ?

While I stood at gaze, partly concealed by the tree against which I leant, Sybil

suddenly sprang to her feet, nearly upset-
ting the youth as she did so, and crying
out—"It is a hateful daub, I will tear it up,
and give it to the river-god."

The artist made a gesture as if to snatch
the condemned sketch. "No, no, Miss
Sybil, give it to me!"

"To you! to mock and scoff at it? no,
indeed. Here—River-god!"

And tearing the paper in two, she flung
it into the stream, though I do not know
how she expected a river-god to accept a
drawing, even in *water-colours*, when it was
rent in twain! But her foot slipped on a
pebble, she gave a little shriek, as she
splashed, ankle-deep, into the water. Only
ankle-deep; there was no cause at all for
Mr. Artist's alarm, as he caught her round
the waist, as if he were stopping her on the
brink of Niagara! She shook off his arm

instantly, and as she turned away, with a bright blush, her eyes met mine. She ran forward laughing gaily, and the colour did not deepen, but faded.

"Here is Mite! oh, Mite! come and look at Mr. ——, Mr. —— ?"

"Darrell," said the youth, bowing very gracefully, and with only the faintest sign of embarrassment at being surprised in such very free-and-easy communication with a young lady who did not even know his name!

"At Mr. Darrell's beautiful paintings," finished Sybil, quite unconcernedly.

Now, what ought I to have done? I know what Miss Colvin would have done, if *she* had detected one of her pupils in the act of infringing every law of academic propriety and social etiquette: she would have looked daggers at the male offender, out of her steel-gray eyes—stabbed him dead, as it were, with piercing scorn and reprobation; then, over his murdered self-esteem, she would have marched, without a backward glance of pity, leading away the accomplice of his crime, to condign punishment and a private execution! However, it was not in accordance with my principles of instruction to teach my naughty sister the duty of observing *les convenances* by showing myself discourteous and ill-bred. So, reserving until we should be alone the reproof she had so justly incurred, I addressed her companion with a cold graciousness, though I could scarcely help smiling at the wistful anxiety with which he looked at me, nor the evident relief which his face expressed at hearing no severer utterance than this—

"Are you a stranger to this scenery,

15—2

Mr. Darrell? if so, you will find such a lavish wealth of beauty everywhere, that your greatest difficulty will be in selection."

" I am quite a stranger here," he replied— " quite. I came down for a few days with Lord Radford, and the scenery is, as you say, so very lovely, that I have obtained his permission to remain at the park, during his absence, to take some sketches in the neighbourhood. I was asking your sister's opinion of some of them, when you came up."

" This ground is as yet almost un-trodden," I observed, wondering why he should colour up, and look so confused, while offering such a simple explanation. " You will be quite the pioneer of your pro-fession in this remote district."

" My profession ?" he said enquiringly.

" You are an artist, are you not? I understood from my sister—"

"Oh, ah, yes, certainly. I am an artist, certainly, if you can dignify such performances with the name of art."

My eyes followed his, and lo, to my horror, there was Sybil, coolly "rummaging" in the stranger's portfolio, and turning over one drawing after another, with perfect nonchalance, till she drew forth one which she held up to my gaze.

"Is not that charming?"

It was certainly very pretty, and executed with some grace and finish, although, to my fancy, it lacked the practised boldness of a master's touch. But I gave it its due meed of commendation, remarking, "I see that is not an English landscape."

"No, it is a sketch taken in a Piedmontese valley last autumn,—If you will allow me—"

But I considered that I had "allowed"

quite enough to the claims of politeness, and
that it was time to freeze. "We must not
detain Mr. Darrell, Sybil," I said; "you
will find the best views lower down the
river, round the spur of that hill. We are
too much shut in here, by the wood, but the
scenery a mile or two further is very
varied."

The youth accepted his dismissal at
once, and moved away in the direction I
indicated, with a profound salutation to
Sybil, and a still more reverential one to
me, followed by what certainly did not look
very artist-like, a foreign-looking lad, whom
I had not noticed before, bearing his master's
paraphernalia.

"And now, little sister," I said, as we
crossed the rustic bridge, and passed through
the wicket-gate into the privacy of our own
garden, "I want you to explain how it hap-

pens that I find you alone in the wood, in familiar conversation with a young man whom you did not even know by name, though you seem to have told him yours? Oh, Sybil, my darling! there must, I fear, have been some very grave defect in my method of educating you, when such imprudence as this is the fruit of it!"

The real vexation in my tone chased away the merriment from the girl's smiling lips, and a soft trouble clouded her violet eyes, as she clasped both her hands round my waist, in her caressing, childish fashion, and answered—

"Are you angry with me, sweet sister May? I am so sorry, it was very thoughtless of me, but this is how it happened. I was on the bridge, trying to reach some blossoms of willow-herb that grew under it, when I saw Mr. Darrell, sketching on the

woodside. And he came forward and got
the flower for me, and asked me to look at
his sketch of Lyndon old oak. And 1 told
him I had sketched that very same oak,
and he begged me to let him see it. So I
just ran in to the cottage, and brought out
my sketch-book, and we were comparing
the drawings when you came up ; but of
course, mine was such a daub beside his,
that I tore it up and drowned it. Have I
done very wrong ? do forgive me, dear !"

Of course, I forgave her. I thought it
wiser to pass over her fault, than to give
the incident too great an importance, by
showing how deeply it had annoyed me.
In her innocent artlessness, unmingled as it
is with constitutional bashfulness or shyness,
she seems quite unconscious that society
imposes severer restraints on the intercourse
between youth and maiden, than between

girl and girl, and having hitherto only associated with women, she meets a young man with the same frank "*camaraderie*" with which she would greet a new school-fellow. It is well that Thorold will soon be here to exercise a brother's authority over her. I have no heart to assert rule, when I wish only for the sweet equality of sisterly love, and I know that no severity of reproof would be half so effective with her, as the faintest shadow of sorrowful displeasure on my face.

My spoiled darling! still, I cannot allow her to sit chatting by the river bank with any stranger who passes by, though he be an attaché of Lord Radford's. If it had been the curate, it would not have been quite so bad.

CHAPTER XIII.

RIVALRY IN THE FIELD.

" I AM so glad, Jenny dear, that the school prospers, and that your new partner is so efficient. I am glad too, that you will not remove to Kensington this year, although now the elder girls I knew are gone, and those Mrs. Wilson brought out here are strangers to me, I am afraid I should feel like an intruder, even in Bedford Square."

"Ah, Miss Wharnecliffe, you will not care, I dare say, to revisit the old place again, now that you are so happily settled

here," said my old colleague, looking round
the pretty drawing-room in which we sat,
a few days after her arrival, with the French
windows thrown open to the lawn, gay with
its bright flower-beds, " but perhaps in the
winter you may like to come to town for a
little shopping ? You will find the winter
dull here, don't you think ?"

It was useless to try to persuade Miss
Colvin, that one's own fireside, wherever it
may be, is not less dear in winter than in summer, or, that to one reared in the country,
and loving it as I did, the hoar-frost glittering on the trees was at least as beautiful
to look upon, as the dreary waste of
umbrellas in London on a wet day, or its
November fogs and sludge, or its trampled
and polluted snow. Nor, indeed, would
such comparisons have conveyed any mean-
ing to her, in whom the sense of natural

beauty was not only undeveloped, but actually non-existent. I saw that, although she could appreciate the improved position which my increase of fortune had given me, she thought in her heart, that it was dearly purchased, by exile from the world of shops and omnibuses, in which she rejoiced to have her being, and the complacency she felt in her now undisputed rule over the little kingdom I had abdicated, was mingled with pity for my relapse into the semi-barbarism of country life. I was amused too, even while slightly piqued, at the air of superiority which, now that we no longer held the relative positions of principal and subaltern, she suffered to peep out in her conversation.

"Yes, certainly, things are better for you in every way. I don't think your heart was ever quite in your work, dear Miss Wharnecliffe.

Indeed, you were so very young when you undertook it, you seemed always fitter to be your pupils' playmate than their teacher. You know I often ventured to hint an opinion that our young people were just a little too much at their ease with you."

"They all turned out very well, notwithstanding; but then, Jenny, you were always at hand to supply my many deficiencies."

Miss Colvin gave her little sidelong smile in acknowledgment of the compliment, which was, indeed, no more than her due.

"Yes, they all turned out very well,— for I suppose you consider that Sybil's education is finished now? And, of course, if you are satisfied?—"

"The old reproach!—that I have spoiled Sybil! I admit that I did allow her more

familiarity than was perhaps consistent with
strict discipline; but then, Jenny, the other
girls were not always at school, they had
their freedom in the holidays with their
parents. My poor little pet had no other
home!"

"Of course, you know best. Sybil has
such high spirits; she seems to me to have
grown quite wild; but, perhaps, that is
what young ladies in the country are expected to be?"

Her words annoyed me,—even a little
disquieted me. The "fast" girl had not
yet come into fashion; but nothing could
be further from my wishes than to see my
sister a boisterous hoyden or a romp. Yet,
with her exuberant playfulness and utter
absence of the morbid self-consciousness
with which some young girls are afflicted, I
sometimes trembled lest there might be

some danger of such deterioration for her.
When among her schoolfellows, she had
never shown the least insubordination, the
least impatience of the rules, which, by en-
forcing habits of order,—by regular and
constant occupation, — make school discipline, when not too rigid, so healthy and
calming an influence on girls of her excite-
able and impulsive age.

Had those rules been relaxed too suddenly and completely? Was Sybil really
growing " wild," or was it only formal Jenny
Colvin's prudery that made her fancy so ?

She perceived that her speech had produced an impression,—and tried to heighten it.

" You will excuse me, Miss Wharnecliffe,
will you not? You know I am scarcely
less interested than you are in dear Sybil ;
but I am afraid you forget that she is not a

child now,—she is a young lady"—(Miss
Colvin would have thought it almost an
indelicacy to say " young woman,")—" and,
unless it is the custom for young ladies in
the country—you know best—it is surely a
pity she should be allowed to walk about
alone so much as she does."

"Is that all? Why, Jenny, the girls
around Kelvydon often range the hills and
woods alone.   No one here thinks any
blame of that.   Lassie never goes beyond
a mile in search of some flower or fern,—and
is very rarely alone,—Miss Boyden or some
of Dr. Barnes' children generally accompany
her, if I don't."

"And   that   artist   gentleman ? "—said
Miss Colvin, very softly,—" who joined her
in the wood yesterday ! "

"She told me all about that," I said,
impatiently.   "He overtook her at the

bend of the river, and walked with her just as far as the bridge; and you are to blame that she was alone yesterday, for she asked you to go with her, and you refused."

"My dear, I *cannot* walk with Sybil; she goes over stiles and brooks like—a cat! And it is so uncomfortable for me! The other day we came to such a high gate. She vaulted over it before I could look round, and just as I climbed to the top, and put one foot over the rail, there was the clergyman, Mr. Mervyn, coming straight up the field. It was so awkward for me,—and Sybil only stood and laughed at me."

I could not help smiling myself, as I remembered my sister's gleeful description of poor Jenny's agony and embarrassment, at being compelled to receive the greetings of the dark-eyed curate, in such an undignified attitude as sitting astride a five-barred gate. Miss Colvin resented the smile.

"I see, you do not like me to say a word in disapproval of anything your sister does. It is a liberty, certainly. Pray forgive me!"

"Suppose," I said, rising, "that we go into the hay-field, and see that this wild girl is not getting into mischief, as you seem to think she may? Dr. Barnes is getting his hay in, and he has all our servants and our young people to help, with his own household; it is quite idyllic, I assure you."

"Are you not afraid of hay-fever?"—asked Jane, who supposed that hay-fever was some infectious disease like small-pox or scarlatina.—"Is it not dangerous to go at this time of the year into a hay-field?"

" Why, what time of the year can you go into a hay-field, except when there is hay in it ? No, I assure you, there is no fever there,—so come along."

And, rather reluctantly, my visitor put aside her work, and putting on her bonnet and mantle, accompanied me to the doctor's meadow, which lay between his house and the river, just outside the town.

The amateur hay-makers had assembled in full force, as their services were to be rewarded with tea, and " syllabub " a little later. The sun was already low, and there had been a pleasant breeze all day. It was a very lively picture. Here and there a knot of youths stood lazily watching the proceedings, in the shade of the alders by the river bank, while near them a row of young girls, affecting total unconsciousness of their presence, tossed over the swathes

16—2

with forks, displaying to the greatest advantage — and, of course, with equal unconsciousness,—their " fair turned arms and
slender waists," while both groups were
intently watched by Miss Henny, sitting
on a hay-cock beside Mrs. Barnes, a quiet,
good-natured lady, whose chief pride was
in the neatness of her house, and the
spotlessness of her children's frocks,—in
which she received no sympathy from
Henny, who always declared that a tidy
infant was no better than a doll, and that
to wash the dirt off a child's face (especially
if a boy) was to brush the bloom off a
plum, or the down off a butterfly ! Half
the juveniles of Kelvydon, of all classes,
seemed to have gathered in the Doctor's
field, and the uproar was wonderful, as they
rolled about in the hay, piling it over one
another's heads, laughing and screaming.

The inevitable curate, of course, was there, and came forward to meet me, and arrange a shady seat for me beside Miss Hogge.

But where was Sybil ?   I had not long to seek her.   At the extreme end of the field, a waggon came slowly towards us, piled "Pelion upon Ossa," with its fragrant burthen, and, perched on the very top, sat my sister,—a throned Harvest Queen. She held in her arms Dr. Barnes' youngest son, a boy of four years old, whose wide blue eyes were solemn with terror and triumph, as he clung closely to his laughing companion. Round her hat she wore a garland of wild briony, which she had snatched from the hedge, and the green tendrils seemed playing with her hair, that fell from its usually well ordered braids round her flushed cheek and smiling eyes.   However

shocking to Miss Colvin's ideas of decorum
must have been this vision of a "young
lady" riding in a hay-cart, there was
nothing of incongruity in it to me, for her
manner was so entirely that of frank,
girlish enjoyment, without a spark of self-
consciousness or coquetry.

Even Mr. Mervyn seemed to feel that,
for he went forward to address her, with
none of his usual languishing sentimental
air,—and even Henny glanced at her, and
forgot to sneer.

The waggon was stopped, and the younger
members of our party crowded eagerly
round it.

"Put me up !—put me up !—and me !—
and me !—it is my turn !—Sybil, take me !"
To which appeals Sybil had the audacity to
reply,—

"I want.Miss Colvin ! somebody hand me
up Miss Colvin !"

There was a general laugh, less at the proposal, than at the disgust depicted on Jenny's countenance. The children waxed clamorous, and one little thing pleaded so earnestly with me to take her up, and ride with her, that, partly to countenance my sister—partly, I fear, in defiance of her reprover, I suffered Dr. Barnes and Mr. Mervyn to lift me up, and placed myself beside her, with little Amy Weston on my lap, and so we made a triumphal procession round the field, Sybil's pure voice making the woodlands ring with a noble harvest hymn. Suddenly she stopped.

"Oh, Mite, there's Mr.—— there's Colonel Brereton coming! Make them put me down. Carter! carter! stop! put me down, please."

As I sat fronting her, with the little girl on my knee, while two little boys hung

round my neck, I could not turn my head
in the direction to which she was looking ;
but I noticed the rich crimson that mounted
to her forehead, and the bashful droop of
the white eyelids over eyes that the moment
before had glanced laughing defiance at all
beholders.

The waggon stopped.   Colonel Brereton
came to my side of it, and was saluted by
an exulting shout from all the children,
with whom he was a special favourite.

"So this is haymaking, is it ?" he cried,
"I think it looks more like hay marring.
You are a merry party up there !   Can you
make way for a poor cripple ?"

"No indeed," laughed I, "but I will
surrender my place to you, and so will
Sybil, if somebody will help us down."

I turned, as I spoke, to Sybil.   Oh, the
change !   Those downcast eyes, that deepen-
ing blush, the shrinking, modest grace, with

which she half leaned forward to, half drew back from, the arms eagerly extended to lift her from her throne—the arms of the stranger artist, Mr. Darrell.

Like an electric flash came the revelation to me. Adieu, for ever, to my darling's careless childhood, my Undine has found her soul! Mr. Mervyn came up, and held out both his hands to me. I tossed little Amy to him, and slipped down on a sliding truss of hay, more skilfully than gracefully, I fear, and looked back at my sister. Her foot was on the wheel. Already Darrell's arms had touched her slender waist, when she drew back ere he could clasp it, and sweetly blushing, bounded lightly to the ground.

Johnnie pulled down at the back of the cart a huge heap of hay, and with it down tumbled a heap of laughing, shouting children at our feet. Little Tommy Barnes shrieked and howled that his leg was broken, whereupon there was a rush of anxious relatives to the spot, to condole with him ; but when the confusion was over, the waggon moved away, and the fracture in Master Tommy's leg ascertained to have gone no deeper than his knickerbocker.

I found the groups dispersed and reformed. I was once more sitting quietly between Henny and the Colonel. Sybil was far away, with Mr. Darrell beside her, both seemingly wholly engrossed in the arrangement of a bouquet of wild flowers, while poor Mr. Mervyn hovered near them, like a male Peri, if there is such a thing, on the borders of a forbidden paradise.

Colonel Brereton's glance followed mine, and he laughed, and hummed, " ' Oh, the merry merry days when we were young,' but it is not very merry with poor Mervyn, I am afraid."

" Do you know much of Mr. Darrell ?" I asked.

"No, indeed, I never saw him before he came here, but he seems a gentlemanly young fellow enough. Do you wish to know more about him ?" he added, glancing significantly towards Sybil.

" Don't bother !" said Henny, "why cannot you leave the children alone ? If you want to know if young Darrell is suitable for a brother-in-law, I will find out what his fortune is, to a penny, and what his status is, to a bow."

"I have no interest in the subject," I answered, coldly, a little annoyed at her coarseness. "I presume" (turning to Colonel Brereton) "that you consider him a fit member of our little circle, or you would not have brought him to-day."

" Have no fear," he answered, " he knows

some friends of mine in the North, to whose houses no one would be admitted without sufficient guarantee for all social proprieties. Even Mrs. Stacy has ventured to invite him to her archery-party and dance on the tenth. By the way, that reminds me that I undertook to deliver certain notes of hers to you, Miss Wharnecliffe, and to Miss Henny."

So saying he handed us our respective notes. Henny read hers with a derisive smile.

"This is your invitation, Johnnie, I know," said she; "I should never have been invited but for you."

Colonel Brereton looked rather guilty.

"That is unfair, Miss Henny. If you will suspect that some extraneous influence has been brought to bear on Mrs. Stacy, why should it not have been the Admiral's, your old friend, you know?"

"My friend! pooh! as if that old goose ever had a voice in any matter, or could make it heard if he had. I know as well as if I had heard you, how you argued Madame Stacy into inviting me. It was, 'You cannot leave Miss Hogge out, when you are asking her neighbour, Miss Wharne-cliffe. She will be offended, and you never can tell what she may say or do, if you put her out; it is merely a civility that will cost you nothing, for she never goes out, and she won't come.' But you were wrong there, Johnnie, for I mean to go."

"Bravo, Miss Henny! it will be quite a triumph, or ought to be, to my cousin, to draw you for once out of your ingle nook."

"Where there is only a grate-paper at this season, or nobody could draw me from it. And I shall not go to the archery, neither. I have done with bows, and all

such 'Cupidities.' I will just look in at the
dancing, and see what the lads and lassies
are about. It will cost me ten shillings for
a fly, May. I will give you and Sybil seats,
and you shall only pay half."

"Thanks, but I fancy the child will wish
to join the other girls at the archery; will
you take Miss Colvin? — A long day's
amusement would tire her, and she dislikes
amusement in the open air."

But Jenny objected that before Mrs.
Stacy's "entertainment" would come off,
she would have "resumed her scholastic
duties."—Poor, prudish little Jenny! such
was her horror of Miss Hogge's brusque,
audacious manners, and daring style of
conversation, that I really believe she would
have sent herself a telegraphic message to
order herself back to town by the next
train, sooner than be shut up with her for

a seven miles' drive,—and most surely, if she had trusted herself to Henny's tender mercies, she would have been tormented without intermission all the way to Plaistow, and back.

"Well, May Wharnecliffe, you must go with me. I am too timid and modest to enter into a ballroom without a chaperone— and it would not be proper,—would it, Miss Colvin? I appeal to you!"

But Jenny only looked down, fidgeted, and smiled, first on one side of her mouth, then on the other; while Henny twinkled mischievously at her, and resumed—

"Well, May, you don't care more for the bows than I do; why not let Sybil, with all her finery, go the day before? Mrs. Stacy, I know, has told you that she may always have a bed in Constance's dressing-room."

"We will settle that later," I replied, for

at that moment Sybil joined us, followed
by her brace of admirers. I looked very
intently at the two young men, as they
came up, trying to realise to myself which of
them would be my choice were I in Lassie's
place. Both were young, both good-looking,
both had the air and style of gentlemen,
although in Mr. Mervyn's case there was
just the slightly professional tinge which
makes it sometimes difficult at a passing
glance to distinguish between the Apos-
tolical Isaac of the University and the
Diocese, and his Ishmaelite brother of the
Chapel and Synod.

Julius Mervyn was as good-looking as a
well-made figure (and coat), neat hands
and feet, white teeth, and large black eyes,
could make a man of six-and-twenty. Although reserved, even timid, in general
society, he possessed a full average of intel-

ligence and culture ; and if fond—as young men will be—of exhibiting his white teeth and his fine eyes, when answering smiles and glances would show appreciation of such personal advantages, such allurements never detained him from graver and sadder duties ; no one could truly say of him that he was oftener to be found at rich men's feasts than beside the sick beds of the poorest of his flock.

Mr. Darrell, although he looked younger than the Curate by perhaps three or four years, showed, by the ease and grace of his manner, that he was older in intercourse with the world. Perhaps, thought I, he owes this to having been brought, in the course of his professional pursuits, into more frequent contact with persons of higher position than his own ? He was not very tall, but slight and graceful, with that indefinable look of inherent, instinctive refinement that it is difficult not to accept as a guarantee of good-breeding and good birth. I suppose he would be called handsome—his features were very regular, he had fair hair, and a silky moustache that did duty for the whiskers that had not yet put in an appearance. But his light gray eyes had a wandering, uncertain expression, and the curve of his lips—if, as Mrs. Stacy would say, " decidedly aristocratic,"—was a little supercilious too.

I ended my silent comparison of the pair by this reflection :—If I were a young girl, with those two young men for my wooers, I should *admire* Mr. Darrell the most, and *trust* Mr. Mervyn more. As for loving either of them,— But then neither of them in the least resembles my one ideal of manly perfection !

CHAPTER XIV.

ENDS IN SNUFF.

" AND so that is really all you know of him; that he was engaged by Lord Radford to paint some pictures,—or hang some pictures, was it ?—at Lyndon Park; that he has good looks and good manners, and visits somebody whom Johnnie knows ? And on the strength of this, you let him philander after your pretty sister day after day, until Sybil is as much in love with him as you were with Thorold Challoner at her age. Really, May Wharnecliffe, for an instructress of youth of ten years' practice,

17—2

I must say your system of government is
wonderfully lax, and if it had not been for
Miss Colvin, half your pupils in Bedford
Square would have eloped before the first
vacation with your riding masters, or your
music masters, while you were dreaming
your own love-dreams."

"But what can I do, Miss Henny?"
I answered, a little fretfully, "I can no
more help Mr. Darrell's admiring Sybil,
than I can help Mr. Mervyn's doing so.
Am I to be rude to every man who
speaks to her until I can find out what
balance he has at his banker's? I have
never once asked young Darrell into my
house, but I cannot prevent him from
setting up that easel of his on Hartley
Knoll, whence he can see right down into
our garden, and over the garden into the
street, so that Sybil can never stir but he

knows exactly where to pounce on her. It is of no use my looking black at him—he does not care one bit."

"I should think not !" laughed Henny; "your black looks are as terrible as the snarls of Conny Stacy's toy-terrier !— Don't be vexed, dear, I only wished to tease you, of course you can't help it— 'where there's a will there's a way,' and young Darrell would find out the way, bar it as you might. But I'll tell you what— How long is it since that young gentleman first came among us ?"

"How long ?—oh, not more than three weeks."

"A great deal of mischief can be done in three weeks, especially these long summer days," observed Henny, sententiously. "I daresay it is all right, we can all see that Mr. Darrell is a gentleman. I daresay he

is very well connected—though nobody has
ever heard him speak of his family,—and
possibly he is very rich—for an artist!
By the way, how do you know that he is
an artist at all? Now consider, take your
time, how do you know it?"

The question, and still more Henny's
significant way of asking it, disconcerted
me extremely, but I took my time as she
desired, and then replied confidently,—
" Why, we see it, of course; is he not con-
tinually sketching, doing nothing else in
short?"

" Except admiring Sybil," rejoined Miss
Hogge, dryly; " but a man may sketch
without being a professional painter, and
to tell you the truth, Mr. Darrell's paintings,—I have seen one or two of them,—
are not exactly the stuff to keep a wife and
ten children on! but did he ever tell you
that he was an artist, in so many words?"

"I cannot remember that he ever did, but we have taken it for granted, and he has never denied it."

"Not likely that he would deny what gives him such a good excuse for loitering about where he can watch the prettiest girl he has a chance of meeting in his lifetime ! But, May, it was you who first asserted, in this very room, that he was an artist, who had come to arrange Lord Radford's picture gallery."

"So I did; how thoughtless of me to make such a statement. But I think I only said I gathered it from something he had said to Sybil ?"

"Exactly,—and Johnnie 'gathered' it from you, and the Stacys and the Barnes 'gathered' it from Johnnie and me, and so the fact was accepted, 'taken for granted,' as you say, that Mr. Darrell has come here to execute Lord Radford's commission to

paint our scenery, and his presence being
thus satisfactorily accounted for, Kelvydon's
curiosity falls asleep, and he goes out and
comes in among us without further enquiry.
We have got so used to him, and his easel,
and all his paraphernalia of paint pots (by
the way, he has too much of it for a professional), and his little Italian page, who
cannot speak a word of English, to carry
his rubbish.   But Kelvydon is beginning to
open one eye, and smile a little, when
pretty Sybil Wharnecliffe and the handsome artist so often chance to meet ; and,
my belief is, that he is no more an artist
than your cat is !"

"What can it matter whether he is or
not ?" I answered, peevishly, for I was
provoked, and a little uneasy too, at the
malignant sagacity in Henny's eyes.

"If you understood men as well as *I* do,

May, you would know that it matters a great deal. A man who means honourably by a girl, is always eager to tell her and her friends everything about himself, his position, his prospects, his connection; if he is reserved on these points, either there is something to conceal, or he does not think of her as his future wife."

" Oh, as for that, Sybil is far too young for me to give any thought to the subject as far as *she* is concerned !"

" Not younger than you were when you accepted Thorold Challoner."

"That is very different—Thorold and I had been brought up together almost."

" Why, May, are you blind ? Sybil was a child five weeks ago, with no care, no thought, but of girlish fun and frolic; look at her now ! She is a woman ! with a woman's dignity, a woman's bashfulness,

with—(Lord help her!)—a woman's bound-
less credulity, which you sentimentalists
call faith, in the worth and nobleness of
the common-place animal she worships as a
god; and you—you 'never give a thought
to the subject,' whether this idol of hers is
a satyr, a Moloch who will gobble her up,
or a decent image to be set on her chimney-
piece and worshipped by sanction of the
marriage service."

"But I repeat—what can I do? If only
Thorold were here——"

Miss Henny gave a snort of disgust.
"Thorold! and how could Thorold help
you, I should like to know?"

"He might, at least, ascertain who and
what this youth is. But, indeed, even
Mrs. Stacy and Colonel Brereton seem
satisfied that there is nothing objectionable
about him."

"Johnnie only looks upon him in the light of an ordinary acquaintance. Men never concern themselves whether a man is eligible or otherwise, from a matrimonial point of view, unless they have daughters or sisters interested in it. As for Mrs. Stacy, she has heard enough of that little sleepy whisper in Kelvydon, to know that *her* girls are safe from Mr. Darrell, and she wants partners for them and their friends at her ball. I'll tell you what, May, there is only one person who can help you, and that is poor old Henny! I will find out for you who this Darrell is, and if he is playing fair with Sybil. If he is trifling with her, or is not the sort of person you would like for her, I will hunt him out of the country, Italian page, paint-brushes and all."

I cannot say that I was much charmed

with the prospect of Henny's interference in poor Lassie's love affair; I did not doubt her sagacity, nor even her good-will,—but her delicacy! I suppose my countenance expressed some demur, for she resumed, in a wheedling tone, which did not conceal a sneer.

" You fancy I cannot have much influence with young men—I, an old maid, who was never a beauty in my youth. Why, dear, I have the love confidences of all the men in and near Kelvydon for two generations, and I will have Mr. Darrell's before I have done. That is one reason I go to Mrs. Stacy's grand party on the tenth—one of two reasons. I go to vex her, because she would like me to stay away, and I go to watch the new flirtations that are going on :—flirtations that have been in bud a whole season, burst out into full bloom at a dance, like crocuses or tulips that expand in a hot room. I have been very quiet all the winter; I must wake up, or I shall be forgotten. I do not mean the Plaistow or the Kelvydon folk to forget me, so I will go and worry them all round."

" Do not be so aggressive, Miss Henny."

" I must be aggressive, sometimes, or I shall lose my prestige. Mankind is ruled only by love (of themselves) or fear. Besides, I want to see what that goose Conny Stacy is about. She has chosen to fix on Johnnie for her hero—a man old enough to be her father—who is not dreaming of her; and she thinks it pretty to let everybody see how devoted she is, and she is simply disgusting."

" I wonder you should be so intolerant of Miss Stacy's attachment for a man you hold in such high favour as Colonel Brereton. I thought you took a kindlier interest in such matters."

" Not in girls', nor in men's either, except in so far as my sympathy gives me influence over them."

" And pray why do you care for such influence ?"

Miss Henny fixed her eyes steadily on me for a moment before she replied, tapping her snuff-box all the time to some rhythm in her own head.

"I am like the lady, who, when she said that she liked ' the individual man, but not the species,' was told that she liked ' every individual of the species.' I am very fond of men. Men and boys, I like to have them about me ; and how can a woman, poor, old, and ugly, attract them, except by acquiring influence over them, through interesting herself in what they are interested in?"

"But do you find it a permanent influence?"

"By no means, but it lasts my time. There is no pleasure in the society of married men—it is just their wives' company second hand."

"That is an odd sentiment from you, Miss Henny, who always speak of women as men's inferiors."

"Not at all," retorted Henny. "Maria Gibson will tell you that there are insects which take the colour of the leaf they feed on, yet no one disputes that the insect's is a higher organism than the leaf's. My view of women's place in the economy of the universe, is, that they are of no earthly use or significance, except in so far as they serve for the physical, moral, or intellectual

support and development of man ! that they
have no separate or individual value whatever, but are created solely to serve for the
nourishment of the stronger sex, like sur-
plus shoals of small fishes, or swarms of
blackbeetles, or any of the prolific animal-
culæ that devour one another."

I gazed enquiringly at her, doubtful
whether she was speaking in jest or
earnest; but she continued, with perfect
gravity,—

" To illustrate this truth, just picture to
yourself a world without women, and contrast it with a world without men."

" I think both would be equally incon-
venient."

" By no means. You are to imagine a
world in which men—or boys, if you like—
arise from the earth like heads of asparagus,
or any vegetable growth, so as to make

wives and mothers superfluous. That one
trifling difficulty surmounted, the world
would go on just as well as it does now.
There would be kings, courtiers, statesmen,
—lawyers in the courts, for men would quarrel—soldiers in the camps, for they would
fight—even clergy in the churches, for some
few would worship—there would still be
science, literature, and art. Looking on
such a world, you would see it busy, active,
and interested as ever.

" Now picture to yourself the same world,
but with only women in it. Why, at the
first glance, it collapses. What could
women be, or do, in a world without lovers
and without babies ?"

" Well," I said, laughing, " I have no
time to argue that with you to-day, for I
see Miss Colvin in the street waiting for
me to join her."

" I suppose," said my companion, " that
she is afraid to come in, lest I should worry
her. So Sybil has been alone all this time ;
you had better hasten home, lest that ever-
lasting painter should be talking to her on
the bridge again. I advise you to plant a
hedge of furze or holly at the end of your
garden. Love may laugh at locksmiths,
but in his classical costume, he could scarcely
be proof against some nice prickly gorse
bushes. There !" and Miss Henny suddenly flung the contents of her snuff-box
into the face of a hapless lad who for some
time had been peering, unnoticed, as he
thought, through the crevice between the
window-ledge and the slightly lifted sash.
" There !" she repeated exultingly, as the
victim vanished with a howl ; " I've snuffed
him out ! Next time you come, May

Wharnecliffe, you may bring me another box-full. I waste a great deal on those intrusive little *gamins* and it is the only thing they mind."

CHAPTER XV.

BIRDS IN FINE FEATHERS.

A BRIGHT, rainless day, for the Plaistow Manor Archery and Ball ; and a
face, sunny as the sky, looked in on me,
for a smiling farewell, as Constance Stacy
stopped her grey ponies at my door to take
Sybil home with her. It was early, for she
had driven into the town to make some
trifling purchases that had been found
wanting at the last moment, and she was
in a hurry, and would not alight. But
Lassie was ready dressed, and at the first
intimation that the carriage was turning

into the street, she had darted upstairs for her hat and the precious box that contained her evening dress, and she was nodding a hasty *au revoir* to me, as I sat at the break-fast-room window, quietly sewing some lace on the bodice I was to don that night. I stopped her in full flight, and called her back to look at her. Her dress was very simple. A delicate blue muslin, looped up over an embroidered petticoat; a mantle of the same, confined round her lithe waist with a sash; a coquettish little straw hat, with a bunch of blue cornflowers in it. The head-tires of the day were as yet only beginning to bud into the rank luxuriance of frisette and pad, that make our girls' heads now look like specimens of *Agaricus umbellica*; but I made my sister's extreme youth the plea for restraining her from any unbecoming fashion, and her dark hair was

folded closely round her pretty head, concealing nothing of its graceful proportions,
poised, as it was, on her slender neck like a
flower-bell on its stalk. She was far too
lovely to need to do homage to any hideous
fashion to win recognition of her charms.

And yet Henny was right; my sister
was no longer a child. There was a woman's
sweet self-consciousness, the prelude to a
sweeter self-abandonment, in the soft blue
eyes that glanced shyly up at me as she
stood before me. I took both her hands in
mine, and she turned her radiant face aside,
as if reluctant that I should read in it all
the joy and hope that sparkled there from
the depths of the young heart that as yet
had never dreamt of sorrow. There was
such a world of significance in that artless
gesture, that I could not but smile, as I
kissed her and bade God bless her, putting

away from me for the moment all Miss
Henny's ill-boding croaks—but she is certainly right in saying that I make a very
bad *duenna.*

Sybil paused, as she was leaving the
room.

"Am I to tell Mrs. Stacy that you and
Miss Hogge will join her in the evening ?"

"She knows all about it, dear; but, my
pet, do not engage yourself to any late
dances, for we are going home in Henny's
fly, and we ought not to keep her up too
long."

"Oh, do let me stop the night, sister
May," she pleaded; "I may sleep in
Conny's dressing-room."

"No, Sybil, you must positively return
with me."

"Why, Mite ?"

"Because I choose. You will soon be

rebelling against my rule, so I must make it arbitrary while it lasts."

She laughed sweetly. "Oh, you tyrant, I can't rebel, I am too down-trodden for that; only—if you would let me stop, and dance the very last dance, and it is my first ball, you know!"

"But, my darling, I am selfish, I own it; still, I have never yet, since we were orphans, slept one night beneath a roof which did not also shelter you, and I should feel lonely and forsaken."

Back came Sybil with one bound, and flung her arms round me. "You silly superstitious Mite! but I will not forsake you, no, never! I will come back with you and the Bashanite" (so she had nick-named Henny) "like a dutiful sister as I am, without a murmur; but Conny will murmur, if I keep her waiting any longer,

so—one kiss more !" and away she frisked
to her friend, and was rapidly whirled away.

As for me, I sedately finished sewing on
my lace, which Lassie's impulsive embrace
had rather crumpled ; then I went into the
garden, quite sure that that day at least,
I should not be overlooked by Mr. Darrell
with his easel pitched on Hartley Knoll;
and there, as was my wont, I fell a-musing.
What if this budding amourette were, as
the mothers say, to " come to something ?"
What if the stranger, whoever he may be,
seriously woos and wins my little maiden?
And suddenly my heart stood still, as it were,
appalled with a sense of great loneliness.
Thorold not yet come back, and Sybil gone!
oh, would it not be as if my world were
mute, but for an echo, and dark, but for the
dim dawn of a distant day ? My world ?
has not my life been so ?

No, Darrell cannot take my Sybil from
me. For her sake, I yielded up my Thorold
for all these years; she must wait until his
return, at least. I cannot live without *both*
of them. I wish I could have kept her
longer mine. She was all and only mine,
until I brought her here—in the seclusion
of the schoolroom I had no rivals, but innocent, brief, girlish friendships, and surely
she was happy then !

Selfish still, May Wharnecliffe? When my
love comes back, my little sister in her turn,
might complain that I no longer lived only
for *her*.

If only I could believe that young Darrell was fully worthy of her ; I do not know
why I do not like him, everybody else
does ; but he gives me the impression of
having no strength of principle, impulsive
and weak. To be sure, I have seen but

little of him. He always contrives to join
us when the Stacys or the Barnes are with
us, and then it is so easy to fall back a
step, with a murmer or a glance for Sybil.
However, this evening I will study him
attentively. Oh, how I wish Thorold were
here! or that I dared ask Colonel Brereton's
advice, without seeming too familiar and
confidential. Unhappy May! with a lover
too distant, and a friend too near! Only
remains Miss Henny, and she is, at the best,
but a rough counsellor. However, I must
make the best of her, such as she is, since
there is nobody else whom I can consult.

At the appointed hour, I arrayed myself
in lace and satin, looked at myself in the
glass complacently, thought I looked very
nice and not very old, and smiled—wished
Thor could see me—and sighed, and then
went down stairs to wait for Miss Hogge,

who was to join me at the cottage, because
she said the flyman always wanted an extra
sixpence for calling at her house, because
the street was so narrow he could hardly
turn his horse in it.

Punctual to her time, in marched "the
Bashanite," in attire in which her ancestor
" Og " might have been proud to behold her
—(though no ancestor less remote would !)
Her robe was a pink satin, of which the
dull texture and dingy hue spoke of frequent trials undergone in the dyer's vats,
since the days of its pristine glory. It was
trimmed with a profusion of spangles, and
pinned up carefully over a petticoat of
checked linsey, which—well, it would be a
violation of confidence to describe that petticoat, for it was certainly never intended for
exhibition except on a strictly "private
view." A really handsome black lace shawl

draped her shoulders, of which, by the way—
the shoulders I mean —she was still proud.
On her head she wore a hood, very much
resembling a flannel jelly-bag, and in her
hand she carried a band-box.

She stopped short, in the middle of the
room, without taking my offered hand, and
exclaimed—

" Why, goodness gracious ! are the days
of fairies come back again ? At a fancy ball
you might pass for Titania or Queen Mab ;
really, May Wharncliffe, I had no idea that
you were still so pretty !"

" I cannot compliment you on your style
of compliment," I answered, laughing ; "but
since ' fine feathers make fine birds,' it is a
pity that I must moult after to-night."

" Well, never mind, my dear ; luckily for
you, you will always be more prized for
your song than your plumage. Just see
how smart *I* am ! I thought I would show

that conceited Mrs. Stacy for once, that
there were gay dresses worn in *my* family,
when *hers* ‾were probably in shreds and
patches. This was my dear mother's wedding gown."

"Indeed!" I said, trying to look "im-
pressed" and interested, while I inwardly
laughed at the thought of Mrs. Stacy's disgust at such an obsolete garment being
paraded at her elegant fête. But there was
worse in store for her.

"I must show you my cap," said Henny.
"I got it very cheap at Miss Poole's, as it
did not please the lady it was made for, and
she could not make up the materials again.
Look here!"

And she drew forth from her band-box,
with great exultation—a widow's cap!

"But, Miss Henny," I expostulated, "you
are never going to wear that? it is a regular

widow's cap! And with a pink satin dress too!"

"No such thing,· May," twinkled Miss Hogge, as she spread out the long muslin streamers; "it is not a widow's cap now, whatever it was meant to be, and as for the pink dress, why, that is the beauty of it, don't you see?—the effective contrast! It is really good of its kind, and quite a bargain. These caps are always becoming to old women, that is why they are so fond of wearing them. You see, a widow's cap can be worn anywhere, and I could never have got a dress cap of any other fashion for the price."

"True," I assented doubtfully, "but—"

"But I do not mean to sail under false colours, so, lest there may be any genuine widows' caps at the Manor—they flourish about everywhere now—I am going to put this in, just by way of distinction."

And therewith she fished forth from her band-box, a faded blue ostrich feather, which she deliberately proceeded to fasten into the front of her " weeds."

I watched her with stupefaction. To be sure, everybody within thirty miles of Kelvydon knew Miss Hogge and her eccentricities, but there would doubtless be many strangers to-night at the Manor, and I cowered at the idea of making my *début* in the company of such a guy !

However, I dared venture no further protest, for Miss Hogge was quick to take offence, and apt to revenge herself when occasion offered, long after the culprit had forgotten his or her liability to punishment. Noticing that she had some difficulty in giving the finishing touch to her millinery, owing to her having on white kid gloves which were much too large for her, and had the

fingers twisted into little spires at the tips,
I timidly enquired—

"Why do you wear such large gloves,
Miss Hogge?"

"Because, my dear," she replied—calmly
depositing her cap in the bandbox again—
"because a large pair of gloves costs no more
than a small one, and I like to get the full
worth of my money. Come along; there is
the fly at the door."

END OF VOL. I.

BILLING, PRINTER, GUILDFORD.